The Soccer Success Playbook

A Step By Step Guide for New Coaches and Parents Through the Youth Soccer Landscape

Early Age Development Edition

Matthew Eric

Contents

INTRODUCTION

It was a chilly Saturday morning, and the dew still clung to the grass on the pitch. I stood on the sidelines, watching a group of seven-year-olds chase a soccer ball like a swarm of bees. One boy, smaller than the rest, caught my eye. He had a fire in his belly, a determination that overcame his size. Every time he touched the ball, his eyes lit up with pure joy. But more importantly, he was learning. He was absorbing every instruction, every tip, like a sponge. It was at that moment I realized that youth soccer is not about winning. It's about nurturing that spark and helping it grow into a flame.

Over the past two decades, I've worn many hats in the soccer world—player, coach, recruiter, and most importantly, soccer dad. I've placed players in top academies, both in the U.S. and internationally. I've seen them compete in prestigious events like the Generation Adidas Cups, MLS Showcases, and along the way, I've guided a semi-pro team to a national championship in the UPSL Premiere Division. But the most rewarding experience has always been watching young players blossom.

This book aims to be your guide through the often confusing landscape of youth soccer. It's for young players eager to learn, for parents who want to support their children without falling into the trap of unnecessary expenses, and for coaches dedicated to developing future athletes. The focus here is on early development, on mastering the fundamentals that will serve as the foundation for future success. Winning trophies at U6 is nice, but it doesn't guarantee scholarships or pro contracts.

Whether you're an adult, a teen, a man, a woman, or a kid, this book has something for you. For parents, it offers insights into supporting your child's soccer journey without breaking the bank. For young players, it provides tips and drills to help you improve your skills. For coaches, it serves as a roadmap for structuring effective training sessions. Everyone, regardless of their role, will find valuable insights that can help them navigate the world of youth soccer.

One of the biggest misconceptions in youth soccer is that early success guarantees future glory. Parents often spend thousands on elite coaching and travel teams, believing that it will lead to scholarships or professional opportunities. But the reality is different. Early trophies don't translate to long-term success. It's the mastery of fundamentals that sets the stage for future achievements. Skills like dribbling, passing, and shooting should be the focus, not the number of medals hanging on a wall or trophies postured on a dusty shelf.

The structure of this book is designed to guide you through every aspect of youth soccer. We'll start with the basics—fundamental skills that every young player needs to develop. Then, we'll move on to structuring effective training sessions, ensuring that each practice is both fun and educational. Mental toughness is another key area we'll cover, helping young athletes build the resilience needed to handle the ups and downs of the sport. Finally, we'll discuss the role of family involvement and how it can make or break a young player's experience.

Early development is crucial in soccer. Studies show that players who master the basics at a young age have a significant advantage as they grow older. They perform better in games, are more likely to be scouted by academies, and have a higher chance of receiving scholarships. Experts agree that the foundation built in these early years sets the stage for future success.

My passion for soccer runs deep. As both a coach and a soccer dad, I've experienced the highs and lows of nurturing young talent. I've seen the challenges and the joys, the frustrations and the triumphs. This dual perspective gives me unique insights into what works and what doesn't. It's a commitment that goes beyond the field, a dedication to helping young players achieve their full potential.

So, I invite you to dive into this book with an open mind and a willing heart. Let's work together to develop young players who are not only skilled but also passionate about the game. Apply the principles you'll find here, and you'll become part of a supportive soccer community. The goal is simple: to help young athletes develop their skills, enjoy the game, and prepare for a bright future in soccer.

The journey starts here. Are you ready?

1. Foundations of Youth Soccer

I remember one practice session vividly. A young boy, no older than five, stood on the field with his oversized jersey flapping in the wind. He looked nervous, clutching a well-worn soccer ball. As the session began, his anxiety melted away with each touch of the ball. His movements were clumsy at first, but with encouragement and simple drills, he began to find his rhythm. By the end of the session, he was dribbling around cones with a smile that could light up the whole field. Moments like these are why understanding the foundations of youth soccer is so crucial. It's about more than just teaching skills; it's about building confidence and joy in the game.

My journey in soccer has been multifaceted, spanning nearly two decades as a player, coach, and recruiter. I've placed players in high-level academies and seen them compete on national stages. These experiences have taught me that the early years of a child's soccer experience are critical. The foundations laid during this period can shape their future in the sport. This chapter will delve into the importance of understanding age-specific needs, tailoring training sessions, and setting realistic expectations for young players. We'll also explore effective communication techniques to ensure that children feel supported and understood. This is the absolute beginning of the journey and much like any commencement, it is imperative to understand where we start so we can appreciate where we end up.

1.1 UNDERSTANDING AGE-SPECIFIC NEEDS

Understanding the developmental stages of children is key to creating effective training sessions. Children go through distinct phases as they grow, each with its own set of physical, cognitive, and emotional characteristics. In early childhood, ages three to five, children are just beginning to develop basic motor skills. Their short attention spans mean that drills must be simple and fun to keep them engaged. Activities like running, jumping, and kicking a ball help build their coordination. At this stage, the focus should be on making soccer enjoyable rather than on any specific skill.

As children enter middle childhood, around ages six to eight, their coordination improves, and they begin to understand rules better. They can follow more complex instructions and start to grasp the basic concepts of teamwork and strategy. However, their cognitive abilities are still developing, so it's important to keep instructions clear and concise. Drills can become a bit more challenging, incorporating simple passing and dribbling exercises. This is also a good time to introduce small-sided games, which allow children to experience the flow of a real match without the chaos of a full-sized game.

By late childhood, ages nine to twelve, children's physical abilities have further enhanced, and they can start to think more strategically. They understand the importance of positioning, tactics, and can handle more advanced drills. This is the stage where you can introduce more structured training sessions that focus on specific skills like shooting, passing, and defending. However, it's crucial to remember that even at this age, the emphasis should still be on development and enjoyment rather than winning.

Tailoring training sessions to match these developmental stages is essential. For younger children, keep drills simple and engaging. Use games and activities that incorporate basic movements like running, jumping, and kicking. As children grow older, you can introduce more complex drills that challenge their coordination and understanding of the game. Always include breaks and fun activities to maintain their interest and prevent burnout. Remember, the goal is to foster a love for the game while developing their skills not to create the next Lionel Messi.

Setting realistic expectations is another critical aspect of coaching young players. Children develop at different rates, and it's important to focus on individual progress rather than competition. Celebrate small achievements, whether it's a well-executed pass or a successful dribble around a cone. Avoid comparing children to their peers, as this can lead to frustration and loss of confidence. Instead, focus on their personal growth and improvement. This approach not only keeps them motivated but also builds their self-esteem.

Effective communication is key to ensuring that children understand instructions and feel supported. For younger children, use simple language and clear instructions. Break down tasks into smaller steps and use visual aids when possible. Encourage them to ask questions and provide feedback. Positive reinforcement is crucial at this stage. Praise their efforts and achievements, no matter how small. As children grow older, you can start to use more complex language and concepts, but always ensure that your communication is clear and supportive. Keeping communication light and effective with familiarity to keywords and phrases is a positive way of relaying your messages without overcomplicating the discussion. Growing up, my son had one particular coach who coined the phrase "rubbish" to his team. The children at six years old understood that "rubbish" was a funny word, especially the way he would overenunciate and pronounce the "ish" when yelling it across the field. However, it relayed the message that things needed to be done better next time in a particular humorous voice and did not undermine or single out poor play directly. Of course, the word "rubbish" took on new meaning when the team entered its teenage years, but for this example, it was well-suited and lighthearted. It was extremely hilarious to hear a six-year-old during a game dribble the ball out of bounds and proceed to yell at himself, "Rubbish!".

In summary, understanding the developmental stages of children, tailoring training sessions to their abilities, setting realistic expectations, and using effective communication techniques are all essential components of coaching youth soccer. By focusing on these elements, you can create a positive and supportive environment that fosters a love for the game and helps young players develop their skills and confidence.

1.2 Creating a Positive Soccer Environment

One of my favorite memories as a coach was the day our team decided to create a mission statement. We gathered the kids, parents, and assistant coaches in a circle on the pitch. Each person contributed a word or phrase that represented what they wanted our team to stand for—words like "respect," "teamwork," and "fun." By the end of the session, we had crafted a mission statement that resonated with everyone: "To play with heart, respect each other, and always give our best." This mission statement became the backbone of our team culture. It wasn't just a set of words; it was a commitment we made to each other. Establishing team values is vital for any youth soccer team. It helps create a culture based on respect, teamwork, and sportsmanship. Encourage mutual respect among players by setting clear behavioral expectations. Make it known that every player, regardless of skill level, is valued. This approach not only fosters a positive environment but also helps in the personal development of each child.

Inclusivity is another cornerstone of a positive soccer environment. Ensuring equal playtime for all players, regardless of their skill level, is crucial. I've seen firsthand how kids light up when they know they'll have a chance to play. It boosts their confidence and makes them feel part of the team. Addressing and preventing bullying is also essential. Make it clear from the outset that bullying will not be tolerated. Celebrate diversity within the team by acknowledging and embracing different backgrounds and cultures. This not only enriches the team experience but also teaches kids valuable life lessons about acceptance and unity. Remind them that this is not their game, it is the world's game and belongs to everyone in it. The ball doesn't care about color, race, classicism, or money, and neither should they.

Building trust and relationships between coaches, players, and parents is another key aspect of creating a positive soccer environment. Regular communication with parents is essential. Keep them informed about their child's progress and involve them in team activities. Team-building activities can also help strengthen these bonds. Organize events like family soccer days or team picnics where everyone can interact in a relaxed setting. Creating a safe space for players to express themselves is equally important. Encourage open communication and make sure every child feels heard and valued. This builds trust and ensures that kids feel comfortable coming to you with any concerns or issues. Communication is the key ingredient to many success models, and this value holds true here as well.

Maintaining a fun atmosphere is perhaps the most important element in keeping kids engaged and eager to participate. Incorporate fun games into your practices to make learning enjoyable. For instance, games like **"Sharks and Minnows"**

or "Soccer Obstacle Course" can make drills more exciting. Allow time for free play where kids can experiment and explore their creativity with the ball. This not only keeps them engaged but also helps them develop a love for the game. Keeping practices light-hearted while maintaining focus is a balancing act, but it's crucial. Kids are more likely to stick with soccer if they associate it with fun and positive experiences.

One effective way to ensure kids are having fun while learning is to incorporate elements of play into your training sessions. For example, instead of just running standard dribbling drills, turn it into a game where players have to dribble through a maze of cones while being chased by a "shark" (another player). This not only makes the drill more engaging but also adds an element of competition and excitement. Another idea is to have mini-tournaments during training where small teams compete against each other in short matches. I would often take two goals and place them in the center of the field with the backs of the nets touching each other. The players would be put into teams of either two or three teammates and then asked to come up with a team name. I required them to come up with a country to represent and enter into our "World Cuppies" tournament. The object of the game is for the coach to play balls into the field and have the teams compete to score a goal on either side of the net. Once the team scored, they would call out their team name and leave the field, awaiting the next round. This would continue until there was only one team remaining on the field, who would then be declared out of the tournament. Being out of the tournament did not exclude them from being part of the game, as they would now become outlet players who could be used to pass and keep possession for those still on the field. These games can be a lot of fun and give kids a taste of real match conditions without the pressure.

Regular communication with parents can also help maintain a positive environment. Keep them updated on their child's progress and involve them in team activities. For example, you could organize a "Parents vs. Kids" match or a family picnic day where everyone can relax and have fun together. This not only builds a sense of community but also shows the kids that their parents are invested in their soccer experience. Additionally, creating a safe space for players to express themselves is crucial. Encourage open communication and make sure every child feels heard and valued. This builds trust and ensures that kids feel comfortable coming to you with any concerns or issues.

In summary, creating a positive soccer environment involves establishing team values, encouraging inclusivity, building strong relationships, and maintaining a fun atmosphere. By focusing on these elements, you can create a supportive and enjoyable environment that helps young players develop their skills and love for the game.

1.3 BASIC BALL CONTROL FOR BEGINNERS

It's dawn on a summer day, and you can hear the rhythmic tap-tap of soccer balls hitting the ground at our neighborhood park. Kids, wide-eyed and eager, gather for another session. Teaching young players the fundamentals of dribbling is where it all begins. Imagine a child, initially fumbling with the ball, slowly gaining confidence as they master small touches to control it. Start by having them use the inside and outside of their feet to guide the ball in a straight line. Encourage them to keep their heads up, not just to see where they're going, but to begin understanding the field around them. Drills like dribbling through a series of cones can make this practice engaging. Set up a simple course and time them, making it a fun challenge. For younger children, the "Protect The Cone" drill can be particularly effective, combining the basics of dribbling with a playful objective.

Passing is the next cornerstone. To teach basic passing skills, focus on the proper positioning of the foot and body. Have them plant their non-kicking foot beside the ball and use the inside of their kicking foot to strike it. Start with short-distance passing drills. Pair up the kids and have them pass back and forth, gradually increasing the distance. Partner passing exercises can also be turned into a game. For instance, set up small goals and have pairs work together to pass the ball through them, scoring points each time they succeed. This not only sharpens their passing accuracy but also fosters teamwork.

Receiving the ball is just as crucial as passing it. It's the yin to passing's yang. Teach players to cushion the ball upon receipt, absorbing its impact to maintain control. They should use different parts of their body, such as the inside of the foot or thigh, depending on the situation. Partner drills are invaluable here. For example, one player can pass the ball while the other focuses on receiving it cleanly. Another effective drill is the "First Touch Skills Series", which helps players get comfortable with receiving the ball from various angles and speeds.

Ball mastery drills tie all these skills together, enhancing touch and control. Simple exercises like toe taps, where players alternate tapping the top of the ball with each foot, can significantly improve their dexterity. Inside taps, another variation, involve shifting the ball between the insides of both feet. Ball rolls and pull-backs add another layer of complexity. Have the players roll the ball with the sole of their foot, then pull it back quickly. These drills can be done in place or while moving, making them versatile and scalable as the players improve. Dribbling through cones is a staple. Set up cones in a zigzag pattern and have the kids weave through them, focusing on maintaining control and speed.

One particular evening, I recall a session where we combined all these elements into a single, fluid drill. We set up a course where the kids had to dribble through cones, pass the ball to a partner, receive it back, and then shoot at a small goal. The joy on their faces as they successfully navigated the course was priceless. It was a clear reminder that the fundamentals, when taught well, can create not just skilled players, but passionate ones.

Incorporate these drills into your training sessions, and you'll see remarkable progress. The key is consistency and making the exercises enjoyable. When kids have fun, they engage more deeply with the material, and their skills develop almost effortlessly. Whether it's a simple drill or a more complex exercise, the goal is to build a strong foundation of ball control. This foundation will serve them well, not just in soccer, but in any endeavor they choose to pursue.

1.4 Introduction to Game Rules for Kids

I remember the first time I tried to explain the rules of soccer to a group of five-year-olds. We were on the field, and their eyes were wide with excitement and confusion. One little boy asked, "Why can't I use my hands?" It was a simple question, but it opened the door to a world of understanding. The objective of soccer is straightforward: get the ball into the opponent's goal. But for young children, simplifying the rules makes the game approachable. Start with the basics, like explaining that players use their feet, heads, and bodies to control the ball—no hands allowed, except for the goalkeeper. The offside rule can be tricky, but a simple explanation works: a player can't be closer to the opponent's goal than the last defender when the ball is passed to them. Understanding the role of the referee is also crucial. The referee ensures everyone plays fair, like a classroom teacher or a game umpire, making decisions to keep the game safe and fun.

Visual aids can make these concepts clearer for young minds. Use field diagrams to show player positions, highlighting where each player stands and moves during a game. Illustrations of common rule violations, such as offsides or handballs, help children visualize what they should avoid. Visual examples of in-game scenarios, like a player scoring a goal or a defender blocking a shot, can make the rules come alive. I've found that kids respond well to pictures and diagrams because they can see the rules in action rather than just hearing about them.

Interactive learning methods engage kids and make rule-learning fun. Rule-based games and quizzes can turn a dry subject into an exciting challenge. For instance, you could set up a "soccer rules quiz" with simple questions and small prizes for correct answers. Role-playing different positions and scenarios also works wonders. Have the kids take turns being the referee, making calls on plays, and explaining their decisions. This not only teaches them the rules but also gives them a sense of authority and responsibility. Using story-telling to explain rules can be incredibly effective. Create a story where a character learns the rules of soccer through various adventures. This method helps embed the rules in a fun, memorable narrative.

Reinforcing rule understanding through regular practice is essential. Incorporate specific rules into your drills. For example, set up a scrimmage where the focus is on under-standing and applying the offside rule. Based on current US Soccer standards, teaching offsides may be premature at this age but we are only using it as a topic example. Before and after games, take a few minutes to review key rules. Ask the kids questions about what they learned and how they applied it during the game. This repetition helps solidify their understanding. Another effective method is to have "rule of the week" sessions where you focus on one rule, explain it in detail, and then highlight it during practices and games. A great example of this might be keeping both feet securely on the ground during a throw-in.

I once had a player who struggled with the offside rule. We spent extra time during practice using a simple drill where players had to position themselves correctly in relation to the defenders before receiving a pass. Again, this rule is generally not introduced until teams reach full field 11v11 lineups; however, I have found that if this fundamental concept is not properly introduced early, even when irrelevant, it can become a problem for strikers as they develop from U9 through pre-teen. Over time, his understanding improved, and he became one of the most tactically aware players on the team. This experience taught me the value of patience and repetition. Kids need time to grasp these concepts fully. By breaking down the rules into simple, easy-to-understand concepts and reinforcing them through practice, you can help young players not just learn the rules but also appreciate the structure and strategy of the game.

1.5 ESSENTIAL EQUIPMENT FOR YOUNG PLAYERS

I remember once watching a young boy, maybe six years old, show up to practice with a soccer ball that was almost as big as he was. He struggled to control it, and his frustration was evident. It was a simple reminder of how crucial it is to choose the right gear for young players. The right equipment can make a significant difference in their performance and enjoyment of the game.

Choosing the right soccer ball is the first step. For very young players, ages three to five, a size 3 ball is ideal. It's small enough for them to handle and control easily. As they grow, you can move to a size 4 ball, which is suitable for kids ages six to eight. By the time they reach nine to twelve years old, a size 4 ball remains appropriate, though some clubs might start introducing size 5 balls. Always ensure the ball is properly inflated; a soft or overly hard ball can affect their ability to learn and enjoy the game.

Next, let's talk about cleats. Properly fitting cleats are essential for both performance and safety. Ill-fitting shoes can lead to blisters, discomfort, and even injuries. When selecting cleats, ensure there's about a thumb's width of space between the longest toe and the end of the shoe. Cleats should feel snug but not tight, providing good support without pinching. For younger players, consider cleats with a mix of studs that work well on various surfaces, as they often play on different types of fields.

Shin guards are another critical piece of equipment. They protect young legs from impacts during games and practices. When choosing shin guards, look for ones that cover the area from just below the knee to above the ankle. They should fit securely but not too tightly. Some shin guards come with ankle protection, which can be beneficial for younger players who are more prone to knocks and scrapes. Always ensure shin guards are worn correctly, with the protective side facing forward and securely fastened with straps or sleeves. Not wearing shin guards at any of my training sessions was a big no-no all the way through high school. Sure, at older age groups during light training days, I would let players get away with no pads because they were mature and we were not engaging in contact during the session. However, younger players have less maturity, and even a simple drill can lead to a dangerous or out-of-control tackle leading to an unnecessary injury.

Safety considerations extend beyond just choosing the right equipment. Regularly check the condition of cleats to ensure they provide adequate traction and support. Worn-out cleats can lead to slips and falls. Goalkeepers, in particular, need additional protective gear. Padded gloves, knee pads, and sometimes padded shorts can help prevent injuries from diving and making saves. Ensuring all equipment is in good condition and fits properly is crucial for the safety and performance of young players.

Maintaining soccer equipment is often overlooked but important for its longevity and effectiveness. After each practice or game, clean and dry soccer balls to prevent them from deteriorating. Store them in a cool, dry place to maintain their shape and quality. Cleats should be cleaned regularly to remove dirt and grass, which can degrade the material. Periodically check the condition of the studs and replace them if needed. Shin guards should be wiped down and aired out to prevent odors and bacterial buildup. Regularly inspecting all gear for wear and tear ensures that any damaged equipment is replaced promptly, keeping young players safe and comfortable.

For many families, the cost of soccer equipment can be a concern. However, there are several budget-friendly options available. At this age, cleats are essential for growth and development but should not have to break the bank to do so. As players progress through the pyramid of development, they will need better-constructed shoes to keep up with the vigorous training and game schedules. Right now, parents don't need to be concerned with the latest and greatest cleats on the market. Chances are, the player's foot will outgrow them even before they are ready to be retired. This is why using second-hand stores for kid's cleats can be a great way of finding cheap "diamonds in the rough". Take it from me, save money on cleats while you can because it only gets more expensive from here! Second-hand stores and online marketplaces often have gently used equipment at a fraction of the cost. Many communities also have gear exchange programs where families can trade outgrown equipment for the next size up. Prioritize essential items like cleats, shin guards, and a good-quality soccer ball over extras. Remember, it's not the brand or price of the equipment that matters, but how it fits and functions for the player.

In essence, the right soccer equipment is more than just a means to play the game; it's about ensuring young players are safe, comfortable, and able to perform their best. Properly fitting cleats, size-appropriate soccer balls, and comfortable shin guards lay the foundation for a positive soccer experience. Regular maintenance and cost-effective solutions ensure that all players, regardless of their financial background, can enjoy the game. By focusing on these aspects, we provide young athletes with the tools they need to thrive on the field.

2. STRUCTURING EFFECTIVE TRAINING SESSIONS

A few years ago, I was coaching a group of six-year-olds on a crisp fall afternoon. One little boy who was new to soccer and was more interested in the leaves on the ground than the ball at his feet came out for a practice. I decided to turn our practice into an adventure, incorporating games and playful drills to keep him and the others engaged. By the end of the session, he was laughing, running, and even dribbling the ball with newfound enthusiasm. This experience taught me the importance of structuring training sessions that are not only effective but also fun and engaging for young players.

2.1 DESIGNING U6 TRAINING SESSIONS

When coaching U6 players, it's crucial to focus on fundamental movements that build their physical coordination and motor skills. This age group is still developing their basic movement abilities, so incorporating activities like running, jumping, and balancing is essential. Relay races are a fantastic way to engage young players while helping them develop these skills. Set up a simple course with cones and have the kids race each other in pairs. Encourage them to cheer for each other, fostering a sense of camaraderie and teamwork. Obstacle courses are another excellent tool. Use cones, hoops, and small hurdles to create a course that challenges their agility and balance. The key is to keep the activities varied and fun, ensuring that the kids remain excited and motivated throughout the session.

Introducing basic soccer skills at this stage should be done in a playful manner to keep the children interested. Dribbling is a fundamental skill that can be taught using simple drills. Set up cones in a straight line or a zigzag pattern and have the kids dribble the ball around them. Make a game out of it by timing them and celebrating their improvements. Kicking at stationary targets is another effective way to teach kicking skills. Place small goals or targets around the field and encourage the kids to aim for them. This not only helps them develop their kicking technique but also improves their accuracy and control. The goal is to make learning these skills an enjoyable experience, so the children associate soccer with fun.

Keeping training sessions short and engaging is essential for U6 players. Their attention spans are limited, so sessions should last no more than 20-30 minutes. Within this time-frame, include frequent breaks to rest and hydrate. A variety of activities will keep the children engaged and prevent boredom. For example, start with a warm-up that includes running and jumping, followed by dribbling drills, then move on to kicking exercises, and finish with a fun game like "Sharks and Minnows" where they can apply the skills they've learned. This structure ensures that the session remains dynamic and exciting, holding their attention from start to finish.

Parental involvement can significantly enhance the training experience for young players. Encourage parents to partici-pate in drills and activities alongside their children. Parent-child drills, such as passing the ball back and forth or playing simple one-on-one games, can create a supportive and nurturing environment. Family soccer games are another great way to involve parents. Organize matches where parents and kids play together, fostering a sense of commu-nity and shared enjoyment. This not only strengthens the bond between parent and child but also allows parents to better understand the skills and efforts required in soccer, making them more supportive and engaged in their child's soccer journey.

Incorporating these elements into your U6 training sessions will create a positive and effective learning environment. By focusing on fundamental movements, introducing basic skills in a playful manner, keeping sessions short and engaging, and involving parents, you can help young players develop their abilities while having fun. The goal is to foster a love for the game that will keep them motivated and excited to continue learning and improving.

2.2 Effective U8 Training Plans

At the U8 level, you'll find that kids are more coordinated and eager to learn. This makes it the perfect time to build on the basic skills they picked up at the U6 level. Structured drills become more important here. For instance, dribbling through cone mazes can significantly improve their ball control. Set up cones in a zigzag pattern and challenge them to navigate through without losing control of the ball. It's a simple yet effective way to develop their dribbling skills. Passing drills with partners can also be introduced. Pair them up and have them pass the ball back and forth, gradually increasing the distance. This not only hones their passing accuracy but also teaches them to communicate and work with a teammate. Small-sided games are another great tool. Organize 3v3 or 4v4 matches to give them more touches on the ball and a better understanding of the game. These games provide a practical application of the skills they've learned in drills, making the learning process more holistic.

Introducing simple tactical concepts can be a game-changer for U8 players. Start with basic offensive and defensive positioning, which helps to explain where they should be on the field during different phases of play. For example, forwards should stay up front to receive passes, while defenders should hang back to protect the goal. Using space effectively is another key concept. Teach them to spread out and use the entire field, rather than bunching up around the ball. This can be done through fun exercises like "Space Wars" where they have to keep their ball in a designated area while trying to knock others out. It makes the concept of positioning tangible and easy to understand. Simple teamwork exercises, such as passing drills where they have to complete a set number of passes before scoring, can also help them grasp the importance of working together.

Keeping training sessions fun and dynamic is crucial at this age. Kids have boundless energy and short attention spans, so you need to keep them engaged. Incorporating mini-games is a fantastic way to do this. Games like "King of the Ring," where one player tries to maintain control of the ball while others attempt to steal it, can make the session exciting. Reward-based activities also work wonders. Small rewards for completing drills or showing good sportsmanship can motivate them to keep improving. Rotating drills frequently ensures that they don't get bored. For example, spend ten minutes on dribbling, then switch to passing drills, and finally end with a small-sided game. This keeps the session varied and maintains their interest.

Assessing progress is another vital aspect of effective U8 training. Skill assessments can be done through simple drills that measure their dribbling, passing, and shooting abilities. For example, set up a dribbling course with cones and time how fast they can complete it. Individual feedback sessions are also important. Take a few minutes after each practice to talk to each player about their performance. Highlight what they did well and offer constructive suggestions for improvement. Positive reinforcement is key here. Celebrate their achievements, no matter how small, to keep their confidence high. I've found that a simple "Great job on that pass!" can make a world of difference.

In my experience, one of the most rewarding moments was seeing a young player who initially struggled with passing finally get the hang of it. We had spent weeks practicing with partner drills and small-sided games. One day, during a match, he made a perfect pass that led to a goal. The look of pride on his face was priceless. It was a clear reminder of why we do what we do. By focusing on structured drills, introducing simple tactics, keeping sessions fun, and regularly assessing progress, you can help U8 players develop their skills and love for the game.

2.3 STRUCTURING U10 PRACTICES

At the U10 level, players are ready to tackle more advanced skills. Introducing passing accuracy drills is an ideal starting point. Set up targets at varying distances and have the kids aim for them, focusing on precision rather than power. Use gates made from cones to create narrow channels through which they must pass the ball. This not only sharpens their accuracy but also teaches them to control the ball under different conditions. Incorporate drills like "Pass and Move," where they must pass the ball and then immediately move to a new position. This encourages both accuracy and quick decision-making, essential skills for any budding soccer player.

Shooting techniques can now be refined. Start with the basics, like proper foot placement and follow-through. Have the players practice shooting from different angles and distances. Set up scenarios where they need to shoot under pressure, simulating real game conditions. Use drills where they receive a pass and must shoot quickly, helping them develop the ability to make swift, accurate shots. This skill will become invaluable as they progress to higher levels of the game. Defensive positioning exercises are equally important. Teach them to maintain a low center gravity and stay goal-side of their opponent. Use one-on-one drills to practice tackling and interception. These exercises help them understand how to effectively stop an opponent while maintaining their defensive stance.

Team play becomes increasingly important at this stage. Incorporate 3v3 or 4v4 games into your sessions. These smaller games give players more touches on the ball and a better understanding of their roles within a team. Use team-building exercises to foster a sense of unity. Activities like "Trust Dribbling," where one player is blindfolded and guided by a teammate, can build trust and communication. These exercises not only improve their technical skills but also teach them the value of working together. Emphasize the importance of passing and moving, and how each player's role contributes to the team's success.

Introducing strategy and tactics can elevate their understanding of the game. Start with basic offensive and defensive strategies. Teach them how to create space by spreading out and making runs. Use set-piece drills to practice corners, free-kicks, and throw-ins. Explain the importance of positioning during these situations and how to exploit weaknesses in the opponent's defense. Tactical scenarios, where you set up specific game situations, can help them apply these strategies in real-time. For example, create a scenario where they need to break down a compact defense or protect a lead in the final minutes of a game. This helps them think critically and adapt to different game dynamics.

Maintaining a balance of structure and fun is crucial to keeping players engaged. Start each session with structured drills focused on specific skills. For example, begin with passing accuracy drills, followed by shooting techniques, and then defensive positioning exercises. After the structured part, transition into fun games that incorporate these skills. Games like "Capture the Flag" or "Soccer Tennis" can make the session enjoyable while reinforcing what they've learned. Ensure variety in your sessions to keep things fresh. Rotate between different drills and games to prevent monotony. The goal is to create an environment where learning and fun go hand-in-hand.

One memorable session involved a mix of advanced drills and a fun game of "Soccer Bingo." After working on shooting techniques and defensive positioning, we played a game where the kids had to complete specific soccer tasks to fill their bingo cards. Tasks included things like making a precise pass, scoring a goal from outside the box, or successfully tackling an opponent. The kids were fully engaged, applying the skills they had just practiced in a playful, competitive setting. It was a perfect blend of structure and fun, and the smiles on their faces were proof of its success.

By focusing on advanced skill development, emphasizing team play, incorporating strategy and tactics, and maintaining a balance of structure and fun, you can create a well-rounded and engaging training experience for U10 players. The aim is to develop their technical abilities, tactical understanding, and love for the game, setting the stage for their continued growth in soccer.

2.4 BALANCING SKILL DRILLS AND FUN GAMES

One Tuesday afternoon, the kids were dragging their feet and seemed less enthusiastic than usual. It hit me then how crucial it is to balance skill drills with fun games. Kids can get burnt out when sessions are too focused on drills. They need to enjoy soccer to stay motivated. Preventing burnout is vital. If practice feels like a chore, they'll lose interest quickly. It's essential to create an environment where they look forward to each session with excitement, not dread. Balancing skill development with enjoyable activities keeps them engaged and fosters a genuine love for the game.

Creative drills can work wonders. Dribbling relay races are a fantastic way to incorporate speed and control. Set up a series of cones and have the kids race each other while dribbling the ball. Not only does this improve their dribbling skills, but it also adds a competitive element that keeps them motivated. Passing games with targets can make a mundane drill exciting. Use small goals, cones, or even hula-hoops as targets and challenge the kids to pass the ball through them.

This improves their accuracy while making the exercise feel like a game. Shooting contests can also be a hit. Set up different targets around the goal and have the kids compete to see who can hit the most in a certain timeframe. These contests are fun and help them focus on precision and power.

Incorporating play-based learning techniques can turn any drill into an adventure. Adventure-themed drills are a great example. Turn the field into a pirate ship or a jungle, and create scenarios where the kids have to dribble through obstacles or pass to escape imaginary dangers. Story-based games can be equally effective. Create a narrative where the kids are heroes on a quest, and each drill they complete helps them advance in the story. These techniques make learning feel like play, keeping the kids engaged and excited to participate.

Providing feedback and adapting drills to keep them engaging is another key aspect. Positive feedback loops are essential. Praise their efforts and improvements, no matter how small. A simple "Great job!" or "Nice pass!" can boost their confidence and motivation. Adjusting difficulty levels ensures that all kids are challenged appropriately. For example, if a dribbling drill is too easy, add more obstacles or increase the distance. If it's too hard, simplify it. The goal is to keep them engaged without overwhelming or boring them.

I remember one particular practice where we introduced a new dribbling relay race. The kids had to dribble through a series of cones, pass the ball to a teammate, and then race back. The excitement was palpable. They were cheering each other on and giving it their all. The relay race not only improved their dribbling and passing skills but also fostered teamwork and camaraderie. It was a perfect example of how balancing skill drills with fun games can create a positive and productive training environment.

Another example, we used an adventure-themed drill was when I had the kids pretend to be explorers navigating through a jungle. They had to dribble around "trees" (cones) and avoid "wild animals" (other players). The kids were laughing and fully immersed in the game, hardly realizing they were practicing their dribbling skills. This drill was not only fun but also highly effective in improving their control and agility. The key was making the exercise feel like play, which kept them engaged and motivated.

Feedback and adaptation are crucial in maintaining the balance. During a shooting contest, one child struggled to hit the targets. Instead of letting him get frustrated, we adjusted the difficulty by moving the targets closer. His confidence grew with each successful shot, and soon he was hitting the targets with ease. Positive feedback, like praising his efforts and small improvements, kept him motivated and eager to continue. This approach ensures that all players, regardless of their skill level, feel included and motivated to improve.

Incorporating these elements into your training sessions will create a dynamic and enjoyable environment for the kids. Balancing skill drills with fun games keeps them motivated and fosters a love for soccer. Creative drills, play-based learning, and providing feedback and adaptation are key strategies to achieve this balance.

2.5 Utilizing Technology in Training Sessions

I remember one particular training session where we decided to introduce video analysis. It was a game-changer. The kids were amazed to see themselves on the screen, and it opened their eyes to aspects of their play they had never noticed before. Incorporating technology into your training sessions can significantly enhance learning and engagement. Video analysis is a powerful tool that allows players to see their actions in real-time and understand their strengths and areas for improvement. By recording practice sessions and reviewing game footage, you can highlight key moments where they excelled or made mistakes. This visual feedback helps them grasp concepts more quickly and makes learning more interactive. Tracking progress is another benefit of using technology. Apps and software can help you monitor each player's development over time, providing valuable data that can guide your coaching decisions. Interactive learning tools, such as augmented reality drills and gamified training apps, make training more engaging and fun, keeping the kids motivated and eager to learn.

Several apps and software programs can aid in planning and conducting training sessions. TeamSnap is a fantastic app for scheduling and team management. It allows you to organize practices, send reminders, and keep track of attendance, making the logistics of coaching much smoother. Coach's Eye is another valuable tool. This app enables you to record videos and provide detailed, frame-by-frame analysis. You can draw on the screen, add voiceovers, and share the videos with players and parents. Soccer-specific training apps, like TOCA Football, offer personalized sessions and data tracking. These apps provide drills tailored to individual needs, helping players improve specific skills while reducing the risk of injuries. By leveraging these technologies, you can create more efficient and effective training sessions.

Using video analysis can be a transformative experience for young players. Start by recording practice sessions or games, focusing on different aspects of play like dribbling, passing, and shooting. After the session, review the footage with the players. Highlight key moments where they performed well or made mistakes. For example, show them a successful pass and explain why it worked, then contrast it with a missed pass and discuss what could be improved. This visual feedback helps them understand their actions and learn from their mistakes. Additionally, you can use video analysis to track progress over time. Compare footage from different sessions to show players how they've improved, reinforcing their development and boosting their confidence.

Interactive drills that use technology can take your training sessions to the next level. Augmented reality drills are an exciting way to engage players. These drills use technology to create virtual obstacles and targets on the field, making training more dynamic and challenging. For example, use an app that projects virtual cones or defenders onto the field, and have the players dribble around them. This adds an element of fun and competition, keeping the kids engaged and motivated. Gamified training apps are another excellent tool. These apps turn drills into games, where players earn points and rewards for completing tasks. For instance, an app might challenge them to complete a certain number of passes or score goals within a time limit. The gamified approach makes training more enjoyable and encourages kids to practice more frequently.

Incorporating these technologies into your training sessions can significantly enhance the learning experience for both players and coaches. Video analysis, apps, and interactive drills make training more engaging, provide valuable feedback, and help track progress over time. By embracing these tools, you can create a more dynamic and effective training environment.

In our next chapter, we will delve into the core soccer skills that every young player needs to develop. From dribbling to shooting, we will cover the essential techniques and drills that will set the foundation for a successful soccer career.

2.6 Spotting and Developing Talent at a Young Age

Having been around the game for decades and coaching players at various stages of development makes it easier to spot natural talent when you see it. Understanding where your current team talent level is essential to understand where your talented players lie within the spectrum of development. The majority of the concepts and drills outlined so far have been for the youngest and most novice players. As each player moves through the early development years, they slowly start to show their own identity as a player. Where they gravitate on the field, are they more geared for offense or defense, do they like contact or shy away from it, do they like the ball at their feet, do they like to run the flanks or stay central? Most of these questions create answers on their own over time, however, it is still important to allow freedom for players u6-u10 to explore playing multiple positions on the field. Chances are likely that where they initially begin their soccer journeys is not necessarily where they will end up later in life. I have often seen this concept thrown by the wayside and sacrificed for coaches' notoriety and accolades for winning a few more games and maybe even the U6 league championship. We will delve into various pathways and player progression for all skill levels in later chapters but I think it is important to understand that the separation of "natural" skill levels occurs even at the most youthful stages of development. That is not to say if your child isn't a superstar at u6 or u8 that they can't progress into a top player. It is also not to say that if your child is naturally bigger, stronger, and faster than everyone else at early stages they will remain in that top tier as they get older and everyone else physically catches up.

I have seen it time and time again where a less physically gifted young player is not nearly as valued as his larger counterpart. Usually, the coach puts into a game plan of getting the ball to the larger player by playing "boot ball" into open space and having them use their pace to simply run onto the ball and overpower defenders. This does work at these age groups but really can have long-lasting ramifications for the player as they progress to where their size and speed are nullified when everyone catches up. This has been a topic for debate in the US for many years and continues to be at the forefront of our discussions with other topics like "Pay for Play" and the academy structures.

**Size and speed catch up with everyone later in development.
Focus on technical abilities.**

3. Developing Core Soccer Skills

I remember a time when one of my players was struggling to keep the ball close while dribbling. He would often lose control, and his frustration was palpable. One day, during practice, I noticed him mimicking the movements of a more advanced player. He was determined to improve. With some focused drills and encouragement, his dribbling skills transformed remarkably. Watching him gain confidence and control was a rewarding experience, underscoring the importance of mastering core soccer skills early on.

3.1 Dribbling Techniques for Young Players

Dribbling is one of the most fundamental skills in soccer. It's the first step in learning how to control the ball and navigate the field. Basic dribbling fundamentals begin with keeping the ball close to your feet. Encourage players to use both the inside and outside of their feet to guide the ball. This dual usage helps in maintaining control and maneuvering around opponents. One effective drill is the "Cone Weaving Drill", where players dribble through a series of cones placed in a straight line or zigzag pattern. This exercise enhances their ability to control the ball while moving and prepares them for more complex dribbling tasks.

Dribbling in tight spaces is crucial for game situations where players need to navigate through defenders. The "Box Dribble" drill is excellent for this purpose. Set up a small square with cones and have players dribble within this confined space, focusing on maintaining control and changing direction quickly. Another effective drill is the "Rondo" game, where players form a circle with one or two players inside trying to intercept the ball. This game not only improves dribbling but also sharpens passing and decision-making skills. Start by allowing 2 or 3 touches before making a pass through the center of the circle and progress to 1 touch as the players skill levels and confidence grow. Cone weave drills can also be very beneficial. Arrange cones in a weaving pattern and have players dribble through them as quickly and accurately as possible. These drills simulate real-game scenarios, helping players become more adept at maintaining control in tight spaces.

Speed dribbling is another essential aspect of dribbling. It's about maintaining control while moving at high speed. Straight-line speed dribbling is a straightforward drill where players sprint while dribbling the ball in a straight line. The goal is to keep the ball close without losing speed. The "Gates" drill with timed sprints adds an element of competition. Set up small gates made of cones along a straight path and have players dribble through them as fast as they can. Timing their sprints and challenging them to beat their previous times can make this drill more engaging. These exercises help players develop the ability to control the ball while moving quickly, a skill that is invaluable during fast breaks and counter-attacks in games.

One-on-one dribbling drills simulate real-game scenarios where players need to evade defenders. The "1v1 Attack" drill is a great way to develop this skill. Set up a small area where one player is the attacker and the other is the defender. The attacker's goal is to dribble past the defender and score in a small goal. This drill teaches players how to use feints and changes of pace to get past opponents. Another useful drill is the "Shadow Dribble" game, where one player dribbles the ball while another player shadows them, trying to intercept without making contact. This drill helps improve both dribbling and defensive skills. "King of the Hill" is another fun and competitive drill. Players try to maintain possession of their ball while attempting to knock other players' balls out of a designated area. This drill not only enhances dribbling skills but also teaches players to protect the ball under pressure.

Interactive Exercise: Dribble Journal

Encourage players to keep a dribble journal. After each practice, have them jot down what drills they did, what they found challenging, and what they improved on. This reflective exercise helps players track their progress and set goals for future practices. Over time, they can look back and see how far they've come, boosting their confidence and motivation.

Dribbling is more than just a skill; it's an art form that requires practice, patience, and perseverance. By focusing on these drills and techniques, players can develop the control and confidence needed to excel on the field. Whether it's weaving through cones, dribbling at speed, or evading defenders in one-on-one situations, mastering these techniques will give young players a solid foundation to build upon.

I would also try to introduce new dribbling patterns or techniques weekly to have the players master throughout the season. I would start with toe touches on a stationary ball and add one new technique each week. Another example would be "inside outside," touching the ball with both sides of both feet in a small space. As the season progressed, I would incorporate skills that were tailored to the teams level but also challenging them to learn skills they may have seen professional players perfect online or on television. A few good examples of this would be learning the "Messi," which mirrored the way he dipped his shoulder and changed directions in a split second, or the "Ronaldo," where he did multiple stepovers to get his opponent guessing and off balance before moving the ball past them. Allowing younger players the opportunity to master the art of dribbling and not playing so "robotic" is a key element for all players moving forward. Understanding the timing or functionality of dribbling vs. passing will come later in development, but for now, players should be allowed to explore keeping the ball at their feet and becoming as creative as possible.

3.2 MASTERING THE ART OF PASSING

Passing is the backbone of soccer. It's the glue that holds a team's play together. Short passing techniques are the starting point. When teaching short passes, emphasize the positioning of the non-kicking foot. It should be planted firmly beside the ball, pointing in the direction of the intended pass. This stable base ensures balance and accuracy. Next, focus on making contact with the inside of the foot. This part of the foot provides a broad, flat surface, making it easier to control the ball's direction and speed. The follow-through is just as crucial. Ensure the kicking foot follows through in a straight line toward the target. This motion helps guide the ball accurately. Practicing these fundamentals, over and over, builds muscle memory. One effective drill is the "Pass and Move," where players pass the ball to a partner and then move to a new position, constantly staying active.

Long passing and switching play come next. This technique allows players to quickly move the ball across the field, opening up space and changing the point of attack. For long passes, striking the ball with the laces generates the needed power and distance. Encourage players to aim for height and distance by leaning slightly backward while striking. The "crossfield switch" drill is an excellent way to practice this. Set up targets or cones on opposite sides of the field and have players aim to hit these targets with long passes. This drill not only helps with accuracy but also teaches players to read the game and understand when to switch play.

Passing under pressure is a vital skill that separates good players from great ones. The "Pressure Passing" drill simulates game pressure by having players pass the ball while being closely marked by a defender. This drill forces quick decision-making and precise passes. Another effective exercise is the "Pass and Move" game, where players must keep the ball moving under tight pressure, constantly looking for open teammates. These drills help players develop composure and accuracy, even when under duress. By consistently practicing passing under pressure, players learn to keep their cool and maintain possession during real matches.

Combining passes and movement is the final piece of the puzzle, creating fluid and dynamic play. The "Give and Go" drill is a classic exercise that teaches players to pass the ball and then immediately move into space to receive it back. This drill encourages quick thinking and teamwork. The "Pass and Follow" drill adds another layer. After passing, players follow their pass and move to a new position, creating a continuous flow of movement.

The "Triangle Passing Drill" is also highly effective. In this drill, players form a triangle and pass the ball in a specific order, constantly moving to maintain the shape of the triangle. These exercises teach players the importance of off-the-ball movement and help create a more dynamic, cohesive team play. "Box Passing" is a cornerstone of learning how to check away from a defender, create space to receive the ball, open their hips to play the ball into the right direction, and then hit a firm pass using the inside of the foot. Switching directions allows the players to learn using both feet, and progressing to 1 touch "knockdowns" should be the maximum progression for this drill.

Visual Element: Passing Accuracy Chart

Create a chart to track your passing accuracy. Draw a simple soccer field and mark different zones. After each practice, note how many successful passes you made in each zone. Over time, this chart will help you identify areas for improvement and track your progress.

One memorable session involved using these combined drills in a small-sided game. The players were divided into teams and had to complete a series of passes before attempting to score. The focus was on maintaining possession and moving off the ball. The energy was electric as the kids executed give-and-go passes, switched play with long passes, and navigated pressure with quick, accurate passes. The game not only reinforced their skills but also showed them the real-world application of what they had been practicing. Watching them connect passes seamlessly and create scoring opportunities was a testament to the power of mastering passing techniques.

3.3 SHOOTING DRILLS FOR ACCURACY AND POWER

Shooting is one of the most exhilarating aspects of soccer. Seeing the ball hit the back of the net is a thrill like no other. But to achieve that, players need to understand the proper shooting technique. Start with the fundamentals. Ensure that players plant their non-shooting foot firmly beside the ball, pointing toward the target. This provides balance and stability. Next, focus on striking the ball with the laces or the instep of the foot. Striking with the laces generates power, while the instep offers more control. The follow-through is equally critical. The body should be aligned with the direction of the shot, and the kicking foot should follow through toward the target. These steps form the foundation of a powerful and accurate shot.

To improve shooting accuracy, a variety of drills can be employed. The "Target Practice" drill involves setting up targets in the goal and challenging players to hit them. This could be as simple as aiming for the corners or using small cones or markers as targets. The "Corners Challenge" drill adds a layer of difficulty by focusing on hitting the top or bottom corners of the goal. Players must aim for these spots, honing their precision. The "One-touch Finishing" drill is another excellent exercise. In this drill, players receive a pass and must take a single touch to control and shoot the ball. This drill simulates game conditions where quick decision-making and accuracy are crucial.

Developing power in shots without sacrificing accuracy is a skill that requires focused training. The "Power Shot" drill with distance targets is designed to help players build this ability. Set up targets at varying distances from the goal and have players aim for them, focusing on generating power while maintaining control. The "Laces and Instep" power drills are equally important. These drills involve repetitive shooting with both parts of the foot to develop muscle memory and strength. Encourage players to strike the ball with conviction, ensuring that they follow through correctly to maintain accuracy.

Simulating game situations where players must finish under pressure is essential for their development. The "1v1 Finishing" drill is perfect for this. Set up a small area where one player acts as the attacker and another as the defender. The attacker must dribble past the defender and take a shot on goal. This drill teaches players to stay composed and make quick decisions under pressure. The "Close-Range Finishing" game adds another layer of complexity. In this game, players must finish from close range while being closely marked by defenders. This drill helps them develop the ability to score in tight spaces. The "Timed Shooting" challenge is also highly effective. Set a timer and challenge players to score as many goals as possible within the time limit. This drill encourages quick thinking and sharp shooting, simulating the high-pressure conditions of a real match.

I remember a practice session where we focused on these shooting drills. One player, Alex, was struggling with his accuracy. We set up a "Target Practice" drill with small cones in the corners of the goal. At first, he missed repeatedly, growing increasingly frustrated. But with some encouragement and focused practice, he began to improve. By the end of the session, he was consistently hitting the targets, his confidence growing with each successful shot. Seeing his progress was a powerful reminder of the impact that focused, structured training can have.

Close range shooting drill striking with the laces

Reflection Section: Shooting Journal

Encourage players to keep a shooting journal. After each practice, have them note down the drills they did, their successes, and areas for improvement. This reflective exercise helps players track their progress and set goals for future practices. Over time, they can look back and see how far they've come, boosting their confidence and motivation.

Shooting is more than just kicking the ball towards the goal; it's about precision, power, and composure. By focusing on proper techniques and incorporating these drills into training sessions, players can develop the skills needed to score consistently. Whether it's practicing one-touch finishes, aiming for specific targets, or shooting under pressure, mastering these aspects will make them more effective and confident players on the field.

3.4 ESSENTIAL DEFENSIVE SKILLS

Defending is as crucial as scoring goals. The first step to becoming a great defender is mastering the proper stance and positioning. Imagine a player approaching you with the ball. Your stance should be low, with a center of gravity that helps you stay balanced. Bend your knees slightly and keep your weight on the balls of your feet. This stance allows for quick lateral movements, making it easier to shadow the attacker. The angle of your approach is important too. Instead of charging straight at the attacker, approach from an angle to guide them toward the sideline or into a less dangerous area of the field. Always keep your eyes on both the ball and the attacker. This dual focus helps you anticipate the attacker's next move and react swiftly.

Tackling is another essential skill for defenders, but it must be executed safely and effectively. Timing is everything when it comes to tackling. Wait for the right moment when the attacker is slightly off balance or has taken a heavy touch. Use the inside of your foot to dispossess the attacker. This method provides more control and reduces the risk of fouling. One effective drill for practicing tackling is the "Tackling Box" drill. Set up a small box with cones and have players take turns as attackers and defenders. The defender must try to tackle the ball away from the attacker within the confined space. This drill sharpens their timing and technique, making them more confident in actual game situations.

Marking and tracking opponents is another key defensive skill. Effective marking involves staying close to your opponent and anticipating their movements. The "Shadowing" drill is perfect for this. Pair up players and have one act as the attacker while the other shadows their every move. The goal is for the defender to stay as close as possible without making contact. This drill enhances their ability to read the game and stay with their opponent. Another useful exercise is the "Man-to-Man Marking" game. In this game, each defender is assigned an attacker to mark throughout a small-sided match. This drill emphasizes the importance of staying close to the opponent and tracking their movements, helping players develop the discipline needed for effective marking.

Interception drills focus on breaking up play and intercepting passes. One effective drill is the "Interception Lane" drill. Set up two lines of cones about five yards apart, creating a lane. Have players pass the ball back and forth along the lane while a defender tries to intercept the passes. This drill helps defenders anticipate passes and improve their timing. Another valuable exercise is the "Cutting Off Passing Lanes" game. In this game, defenders must position themselves to cut off passing lanes and intercept the ball. Set up a small-sided game where the focus is on intercepting passes rather than tackling. This drill teaches players to read the game, anticipate passes, and position themselves effectively to break up play.

One memorable experience I had was with a young player named Javier. He was eager but struggled with his defensive skills. We focused on the basics: stance, positioning, and tackling. Over several weeks, Jake practiced diligently. We incorporated drills like the "Tackling Box" and "Interception Lane" into our sessions. Slowly but surely, his confidence grew. One game, Javier executed a perfect tackle, dispossessing the attacker and initiating a counter-attack that led to a goal. The look of accomplishment on his face was priceless. It was a testament to the power of focused, consistent practice and the importance of mastering essential defensive skills.

Defending is about more than just stopping goals; it's about anticipation, positioning, and timing. By focusing on these core aspects and using effective drills, players can become more confident and skilled defenders. Whether it's maintaining a low stance, executing a perfectly timed tackle, or intercepting a crucial pass, mastering these defensive skills will make players invaluable assets to their teams.

3.5 GOALKEEPING BASICS FOR BEGINNERS

I remember the first time young Michael put on the goalkeeper gloves. His eyes were wide with excitement, but I could see the nervousness in his stance. We started by teaching him the basics of goalkeeper stance and positioning. The ready position is fundamental. Have your knees slightly bent, keeping your weight on the balls of your feet for quick movements. Your hands should be out and ready, fingers slightly spread, forming a barrier. Positioning relative to the goal and ball is crucial. Always stay centered in the goal, adjusting your position based on where the ball is. This stance allows you to react swiftly to any shot.

Catching the ball is another vital skill for goalkeepers. Start with the "W" hand shape. This means your thumbs and index fingers form a "W," creating a secure net for the ball. When catching, bring the ball into your body to secure it, using your chest as a cushion. Practice high and low catch drills. For high catches, throw the ball above the player's head, focusing on stretching their arms and securing the ball. For low catches, roll the ball towards them, encouraging them to get low and scoop it up. These drills help build confidence and ensure that young goalkeepers can handle shots coming from various angles.

Diving saves are an exciting but challenging aspect of goalkeeping. Emphasize safety and technique. Start with diving to both sides. Have the goalkeeper practice diving to their left and right, extending their arms, and landing softly. Use "Soft Mat" diving drills for beginners. Lay down a soft mat or use a padded surface, allowing them to practice dives without fear of injury. The "Angle Saves" drill is also effective. Set up cones at different angles around the goal and have the goalkeeper dive to save shots from these various positions. These drills build agility and teach goalkeepers how to cover different parts of the goal.

Goal kicks and distribution are essential skills for any goalkeeper. Proper goal kick mechanics involve planting the non-kicking foot next to the ball, leaning back slightly, and striking the ball with the laces for power and accuracy. Practice short and long throws as well. For short throws, use an underhand motion to roll the ball to nearby teammates. For long throws, use an overhand technique, aiming to reach teammates further down the field. The "Distribution Accuracy" drill can help with this. Set up targets at various distances and challenge the goalkeeper to hit these targets with both kicks and throws. This drill improves their accuracy and decision-making in distributing the ball effectively.

Interactive Element: Goalkeeper Checklist

Create a checklist for young goalkeepers to track their progress. Include items like "Perfected Ready Stance," "Secured High and Low Catches," "Practiced Diving Saves," and "Improved Distribution Accuracy." Have the players check off each item as they master these skills. This visual progress tracker can boost their confidence and keep them motivated.

One of the most rewarding moments was seeing Michael's transformation. After weeks of practicing these basic techniques, he was no longer the nervous kid who first put on the gloves. His stance was confident, his catches secure, and his dives impressive. During a match, he made a crucial save, diving to his left to stop a powerful shot. The look of pride on his face was priceless. It was a clear reminder of the importance of mastering these fundamental skills.

Goalkeeping basics lay the foundation for a strong and confident goalkeeper. From the proper stance and catching techniques to diving saves and effective distribution, these skills are crucial for any young player stepping into the role of a goalkeeper. By focusing on these areas and practicing regularly, young goalkeepers can develop the confidence and ability needed to protect their goal effectively.

In the next chapter, we'll explore the mental aspects of soccer, focusing on building resilience and handling pressure on and off the field.

4. MENTAL TOUGHNESS AND SPORTS PSYCHOLOGY

One sweltering summer day, I watched a young player named Zack face what seemed like an insurmountable challenge. Our team was down by two goals, and the clock was ticking away. Zack, usually brimming with confidence, seemed overwhelmed. He missed a few passes and was visibly frustrated. During a short break, I pulled him aside and reminded him of all the hard work he had put in and how he always bounced back from tough situations. With a deep breath, he returned to the field, his resolve evident. He assisted in one goal and then scored another, bringing the game to a thrilling draw. It was a powerful moment that highlighted the importance of mental resilience in young athletes.

4.1 BUILDING MENTAL RESILIENCE IN YOUNG ATHLETES

Understanding mental resilience is the first step. Mental resilience is the ability to bounce back from setbacks, adapt to challenges, and keep pushing forward despite difficulties.

It's a crucial trait for young athletes because sports, by nature, are filled with highs and lows. Whether it's losing a game, facing tough competition, or dealing with personal struggles, resilience helps athletes navigate these obstacles. In sports, resilience can be the difference between giving up and pushing through. It allows players to maintain focus, stay motivated, and continue improving, even when things get tough.

Building mental resilience involves several techniques that can be incorporated into daily routines. One effective method is setting incremental goals. Instead of focusing solely on long-term achievements, break them down into smaller, manageable steps. For example, if a player aims to improve their passing accuracy, start with a goal of making ten successful passes in a row, then gradually increase the number. This

approach makes larger goals feel more attainable and provides a sense of accomplishment along the way. Positive self-talk is another powerful tool. Encourage young athletes to replace negative thoughts with positive affirmations. Instead of thinking, "I can't do this," teach them to say, "I'm improving every day." This shift in mindset can significantly boost their confidence and resilience. Routine-based resilience exercises can also help. Establishing a pre-game routine that includes visualization, deep breathing, and positive affirmations can prepare athletes mentally and emotionally for the challenges ahead.

Coaches and parents play a vital role in developing resilience in young players. Encouraging persistence is key. Whenever a child faces a setback, remind them of their past successes and how they've overcome challenges before. Constructive feedback is crucial as well. Instead of focusing solely on what went wrong, highlight what they did well and offer specific suggestions for improvement. This balanced approach helps them learn and grow without feeling discouraged. Creating a supportive environment is perhaps the most important factor. Ensure that the team culture emphasizes effort, learning, and improvement rather than just winning. Celebrate the small victories and progress that each player makes. This supportive atmosphere fosters a sense of belonging and encourages players to keep pushing forward, even when they face difficulties.

Resilience-building activities can be both fun and effective. "Obstacle Overcome" challenges are a great example. Set up a series of physical and mental challenges that players must navigate, such as dribbling through cones while answering trivia questions. This activity combines physical skills with cognitive tasks, teaching players to stay focused and adaptable. Team-building exercises also play a crucial role. Activities like trust falls or group problem-solving tasks help build trust and camaraderie among teammates, reinforcing the idea that they can rely on each other during tough times. Reflection journaling is another effective tool. Encourage players to keep a journal where they write about their experiences, challenges, and how they overcame them. Reflecting on their journey can help them recognize their growth and resilience, boosting their confidence.

Interactive Element: Reflection Journaling Prompt

Encourage players to start a reflection journal. Here's a prompt to get them started: "Think about a time when you faced a challenge in soccer. How did you feel? What steps did you take to overcome it? What did you learn from the experience?" Writing about these experiences helps players process their emotions and recognize their resilience.

Building mental resilience in young athletes is a multifaceted process that involves understanding the concept, using specific techniques, and creating a supportive environment. Coaches and parents play a crucial role in this development, and incorporating fun, engaging activities can make the process enjoyable for young players. By focusing on these aspects, we can help young athletes develop the mental toughness they need to succeed on and off the field.

4.2 HANDLING GAME-DAY PRESSURE

One Saturday morning, I watched a young player named Ethan visibly tense up as the game began. He had been practicing hard all week, but the pressure seemed to overwhelm him. Understanding where this pressure comes from can help both the player and the coach manage it effectively. Performance anxiety is a common source of game-day pressure. Young athletes often worry about making mistakes or not living up to expectations. This anxiety can manifest in various ways, from physical symptoms like sweating and shaking to mental blocks that affect their performance. Expectations from parents and coaches can also add to the pressure. When kids feel that they must perform well to please their parents or earn their coach's approval, it can weigh heavily on them. Additionally, pressure from teammates can be a significant factor. Kids don't want to let their team down, and the fear of making a mistake in front of peers can be daunting.

Establishing pre-game routines can significantly reduce this anxiety. Warm-up exercises are a great starting point. A consistent warm-up routine helps players focus and get into the right mindset. It's not just about stretching and jogging; it's about creating a sense of readiness. Breathing techniques can also be incredibly effective. Teach players to take slow, deep breaths to calm their nerves. This simple act can help reduce anxiety and improve focus. Visualization practices are another powerful tool. Encourage players to close their eyes and visualize themselves making successful plays. This mental rehearsal can build confidence and prepare them for the game. Visualization involves imagining the game in vivid detail—seeing the field, feeling the ball, hearing the crowd. It's like a mental dress rehearsal that sets the stage for the actual performance.

During the game, it's crucial to have strategies for managing pressure. Focusing on the present moment can make a big difference. Teach players to concentrate on the current play rather than worrying about the outcome. This mindfulness approach helps them stay grounded and perform better. Positive affirmations can also be a game-changer. Encourage players to use phrases like "I've got this" or "I'm ready" to boost their confidence. These affirmations can counteract negative thoughts and keep them focused. Resetting after mistakes is another vital strategy. Mistakes are inevitable, but how players react to them matters. Encourage them to shake off errors quickly and focus on the next play. A simple routine, like taking a deep breath or giving themselves a quick pep talk, can help reset their mindset and keep their performance on track.

Post-game reflection is an essential part of the learning process. Analyzing performance in a positive light helps players understand what they did well and what needs improvement. Encourage them to focus on their strengths and celebrate small victories. This positive reinforcement builds confidence and motivation. Identifying areas for improvement is equally important. Help players see mistakes as learning opportunities rather than failures. Discuss what they can do differently next time and set specific goals for improvement. Celebrating small victories is crucial for maintaining motivation. Whether it's a well-executed pass or a moment of good sportsmanship, recognizing these moments helps players see their progress and stay motivated.

Interactive Element: Post-Game Reflection Exercise

Encourage players to engage in post-game reflection by answering these questions in their journal: "What went well during the game? What didn't go as planned? What can I work on for the next game?" This exercise helps players process their experiences and learn from them.

Managing game-day pressure involves understanding its sources and implementing strategies to cope with it. Establishing pre-game routines, using in-game strategies, and engaging in post-game reflection can help young athletes handle pressure effectively. By focusing on these aspects, we can create a supportive environment that enables players to perform at their best and enjoy the game.

4.3 VISUALIZATION TECHNIQUES FOR SUCCESS

One late afternoon, I watched a young player named Kevin sit quietly on the bench, eyes closed, and hands clasped. Curious, I asked him what he was doing. "I'm seeing myself score a goal," he replied. That game, Kevin did score, and he credited his visualization for giving him the confidence. Visualization is a powerful tool that can enhance performance and build confidence. By mentally rehearsing skills, athletes can prepare their minds for the physical actions they need to perform. Visualization reduces pre-game anxiety by creating a sense of familiarity with the desired outcomes. When players imagine themselves executing successful plays, they feel more prepared and less anxious.

To practice effective visualization, start by finding a quiet place free from distractions. Sit or lie down comfortably, close your eyes, and take a few deep breaths to relax. Begin by imagining a successful play. Picture yourself dribbling past an opponent, making a precise pass, or scoring a goal. Visualize every detail—the feel of the ball at your feet, the movement of your body, the sound of the crowd. Incorporate all your senses into the visualization. Imagine the sight of the field, the sound of the whistle, the smell of the grass, and even the taste of the air. This multi-sensory approach makes the visualization more vivid and effective.

Overcoming obstacles is another crucial aspect of visualization. Imagine facing a challenging scenario, like being closely marked by a defender or taking a crucial penalty kick. Visualize how you would overcome these obstacles with calm and confidence. See yourself making quick decisions, staying composed, and executing the play successfully. This mental rehearsal prepares you for real-game situations, making it easier to handle pressure and adversity.

Incorporating visualization into your routine can make a significant difference in your performance. Make it a part of your daily training sessions. Spend five to ten minutes each day visualizing successful plays and scenarios. Combine visualization with physical practice. After visualizing a skill, practice it on the field. This combination reinforces the mental and physical aspects of the skill, making it more ingrained in your muscle memory. Consistency is key. The more regularly you practice visualization, the more effective it becomes.

Many professional athletes use visualization to succeed. Wayne Rooney, for example, was known for picturing game scenarios the night before a match. He imagined scoring goals, making assists, and leading his team to victory. This mental preparation gave him confidence and clarity on the field. Similarly, Mia Hamm used visualization to prepare for crucial moments in her career. She would imagine herself scoring goals in high-pressure situations, which helped her stay composed and focused during actual games. These athletes credit visualization for their success, highlighting its impact on game performance.

Visualization is a powerful technique that can enhance performance, build confidence, and reduce anxiety. By mentally rehearsing skills, imagining successful plays, and incorporating all senses into the visualization, athletes can prepare themselves for real-game situations. Making visualization a regular part of training and combining it with physical practice can significantly improve performance. The success stories of professional athletes like Wayne Rooney and Mia Hamm demonstrate the effectiveness of this technique.

4.4 STAYING MOTIVATED THROUGHOUT THE SEASON

I recall a season when our team started strong but hit a rough patch midway. The players' spirits began to wane, and I realized we needed to refocus on goal-setting to keep everyone motivated. Setting long-term and short-term goals can make a significant difference. Short-term goals are like stepping stones. They provide immediate targets that are achievable within a few practices or games. For instance, a short-term goal could be improving dribbling skills by completing a specific drill without losing control. These goals offer quick wins and keep players engaged. On the other hand, long-term goals provide a vision for the future. They are aspirations like becoming a better team player or mastering complex techniques. These goals give players something to strive for over the entire season, creating a sense of purpose and direction.

Keeping training sessions engaging is another crucial aspect of maintaining motivation. Rotating drill types can prevent monotony. Imagine starting with dribbling drills on Monday, switching to passing exercises on Wednesday, and focusing on shooting techniques on Friday. This rotation keeps things fresh and ensures that all skills are covered. Introducing new challenges can also spark excitement. Set up obstacle courses that test agility or create small-sided games with specific rules. These new challenges push players out of their comfort zones and keep them eager to learn. Fun competitions within the team are another great way to maintain interest. Organize mini-tournaments or skill challenges where players can compete in a friendly environment. These competitions foster a sense of camaraderie and make training sessions more enjoyable.

Celebrating milestones is essential for keeping motivation high. Team celebrations can be simple yet effective. After achieving a team goal, like winning a match or completing a challenging drill, take a moment to celebrate together. This could be a cheer, a group photo, or a fun activity. Individual recognition is equally important. Highlighting a player's improvement or effort in front of the team can boost their confidence and motivation. Tracking progress visibly can also make a big difference. Use charts or boards to display each player's achievements and improvements. This visual representation of progress encourages players to keep pushing themselves and provides a sense of accomplishment.

Maintaining a positive attitude is the glue that holds everything together. Encouraging positive thinking can transform a player's mindset. Teach them to focus on what they can control and stay optimistic, even when things get tough. Overcoming negative self-talk is another critical aspect. Help players identify and challenge negative thoughts. For instance, if a player thinks, "I can't do this," encourage them to reframe it to, "I'm still learning, and I'll get better with practice." Creating a positive team culture is essential for sustaining motivation. Foster an environment where players support each other, celebrate each other's successes, and work together towards common goals. This positive atmosphere not only keeps players motivated but also builds strong team bonds.

One season, we introduced a "Player of the Week" award. Each week, we recognized a player who had shown exceptional effort, improvement, or sportsmanship. The kids were thrilled and worked hard to earn the title. It was incredible to see how this simple act of recognition boosted their motivation and performance. Another time, we set up a progress board where players could track their achievements. They loved seeing their progress visually, and it motivated them to keep improving. These experiences reinforced the importance of celebrating milestones and maintaining a positive attitude throughout the season.

Staying motivated throughout the season requires a combination of goal-setting, engaging training sessions, celebrating milestones, and maintaining a positive attitude. By focusing on these elements, you can create a supportive and motivating environment that keeps young athletes eager to learn and improve.

4.5 DEALING WITH SETBACKS AND FAILURES

One rainy afternoon, our team lost a crucial match. The kids were drenched, not just with rain but with disappointment. We huddled together, and I told them that failure is a normal part of sports and life. It's an opportunity for growth, not something to fear. Mistakes on the field teach us valuable lessons. Each missed pass, each failed shot, and every defensive lapse is a chance to learn and improve. Embracing challenges, rather than shying away from them, builds character and resilience. It's essential to help young athletes understand that setbacks are not the end but a stepping stone to success.

Overcoming setbacks requires practical strategies that can turn the tide. Reflecting on what went wrong is the first step. Encourage players to analyze their performance objectively. What could they have done differently? What skills need improvement? This reflection helps them understand their mistakes without dwelling on them. Creating a plan for improvement comes next. Set specific, actionable goals to address the areas that need work. Whether it's practicing a particular drill or focusing on fitness, having a plan provides direction and motivation. Seeking support from coaches and teammates is also crucial. A supportive network can offer valuable feedback, encouragement, and different perspectives that might not be apparent to the player.

Fostering a growth mindset is pivotal in helping young athletes deal with setbacks. Emphasizing effort over talent changes the narrative. It's not about being the best naturally; it's about working hard and improving continuously. Celebrate the effort they put into practice and games, not just the outcomes. Encouraging curiosity and a love for learning also contributes to a growth mindset. Teach players to ask questions, seek new techniques, and be open to new ideas. Resilience-building affirmations can reinforce this mindset. Phrases like "I grow with every challenge" or "Effort makes me stronger" can shift their focus from failure to growth.

Emotional support plays a significant role in helping young players cope with setbacks. Open communication with coaches and parents is vital. Create an environment where players feel safe to express their feelings and concerns. This openness fosters trust and helps them process their emotions constructively. Peer support networks are equally important. Encourage team bonding activities where players support each other. Knowing that their teammates have their back can boost morale and resilience. In some cases, professional support might be needed. If a player is struggling significantly, consider involving a sports psychologist or counselor who can provide specialized guidance and support.

One season, a young player named Jake faced a tough period after a string of poor performances. His confidence was shattered, and he considered quitting. We spent time reflecting on his games, identifying specific areas for improvement. Jake created a plan to work on his dribbling and passing, setting small, achievable goals. With the support of his teammates and positive affirmations, he slowly regained his confidence and by the end of the season, Jake was not only performing better but also enjoying the game more. His journey highlighted the power of a growth mindset and the importance of emotional support in overcoming setbacks.

Dealing with setbacks and failures is an integral part of sports. Normalizing failure, implementing practical strategies to bounce back, fostering a growth mindset, and providing emotional support are all crucial elements in helping young athletes navigate these challenges. These lessons extend beyond the field, teaching them resilience and perseverance that will serve them well in all aspects of life.

5. Position-Specific Training

When I first started coaching, one of the most enlightening experiences was watching a young forward named Charles evolve. He had raw talent but lacked understanding of his role on the field. One game, he made a perfect diagonal run, received a through ball, and scored. It was a moment of realization for both of us—the importance of understanding the roles and responsibilities of each position. Charles is now being recruited by professional teams and D1 schools all over the country. This chapter focuses on forwards, the goal-scorers and opportunity creators of the team.

5.1 Roles and Responsibilities of Forwards

The primary objective of forwards is straightforward yet multifaceted: score goals and create opportunities. As a forward, positioning for goal-scoring opportunities is crucial. You must always be alert, ready to exploit any defensive gaps. Position yourself near the opponent's goal, but be mindful of the offside rule. This means staying level with or behind the last defender until the ball is played. It's a delicate balance, but with practice, it becomes second nature. Another key aspect is making runs behind the defense. Timing is everything here. Wait for the right moment, then sprint into space, giving your teammates a clear target for their passes. Equally important is holding up the ball to bring teammates into play. When you receive the ball with your back to the goal, shield it from defenders and look for passing options. This not only retains possession but also allows your team to advance up the field in support.

Movement off the ball is another critical skill for forwards. It's not just about what you do when you have the ball, but also how you move when you don't. Diagonal runs can stretch the defense and create space for you and your teammates. By running diagonally, you pull defenders out of position, opening up gaps that can be exploited. Checking back to receive the ball is also key for any top striker. . Drop into the midfield to collect the ball, then turn and drive forward. This keeps defenders guessing and disrupts their marking. Timing your runs to stay onside is a skill that requires practice and awareness. Always keep an eye on the defensive line and time your runs to perfection. A well-timed run can be the difference between a goal and an offside call.

Finishing techniques are where the magic happens. One-touch finishing drills are excellent for developing quick, decisive shooting. In these drills, you receive a pass and shoot in one fluid motion. This mimics game situations where you have little time to control the ball before shooting. Shooting from different angles is another vital skill. Practice taking shots from various positions around the penalty area, focusing on accuracy and power. This prepares you for the unpredictable nature of real games. Volleys and half-volleys are also crucial. These require impeccable timing and technique. Set up drills where you receive a lofted pass and strike the ball before it touches the ground. This not only improves your skill but also boosts your confidence in taking on challenging shots.

Forwards also play a crucial role in defending from the front. Pressing opponents high up the pitch can disrupt their build-up play and create scoring opportunities for your team. Closing down defenders quickly forces them to make hurried decisions, increasing the likelihood of errors. Coordinate with your teammates to ensure collective pressing. This means moving as a unit to cut off passing lanes and trap opponents. Forcing errors and turnovers can lead to quick counter-attacks and goal-scoring opportunities. It's not just about scoring; it's about contributing to the team's overall strategy.

Interactive Element: Forward Positioning Drill

Set up a small-sided game focusing on forward positioning. Divide players into two teams and mark out a smaller field. The forwards' objective is to position themselves for goal-scoring opportunities and practice making runs behind the defense. Use cones to mark the defensive line and emphasize timing runs to stay onside. Rotate players so everyone gets a chance to play as a forward. I continue to emphasize offsides as it is crucial for a striker's natural progression, even if the concept isn't practiced at the very early stages of u6-u8.

Charle's development as a forward was a testament to the power of understanding and practicing these roles and responsibilities. He went from a player who relied solely on his natural talent to one who understood the intricacies of positioning, movement, and finishing. Watching him make those perfectly timed runs, holding up the ball to bring others into play, and pressing opponents high up the pitch was incredibly rewarding. The transformation was not just in his skill level, but in his confidence and understanding of the game.

By focusing on these aspects, you can develop into a forward who not only scores goals but also creates opportunities and contributes to the team's overall success. Whether it's making a perfectly timed run, finishing a difficult volley, or pressing high up the pitch, mastering these skills will make you an invaluable asset to your team.

5.2 MIDFIELD MASTERY: TECHNIQUES AND STRATEGIES

Midfielders are the backbone of any soccer team, acting as the crucial link between defense and attack, no matter what style or tactical formation is being used. Their core responsibilities are diverse, requiring a balance of offensive and defensive duties. As a midfielder, your primary role is to connect the defense with the attack. When your team has possession, you need to move the ball efficiently from the backline to the forwards. This involves quick, accurate passes and a keen sense of positioning. Midfielders also control the tempo of the game. If the team needs to slow down and maintain possession, it's your job to recycle the ball and keep it moving. On the flip side, when a quick counterattack is possible, you need to recognize that moment and act swiftly. Supporting both forward and defensive plays is another key responsibility. When the team is attacking, you should be ready to make forward runs, support the forwards, and be available for a pass. Defensively, you need to track back, mark opponents, and help break up the opposition's play.

Passing and distribution are vital skills for any midfielder. The ability to see the field and execute precise passes can make or break your team's play. Practicing "through ball" drills can help you develop the vision and timing needed to split defenses. Set up scenarios where you have to thread the ball between defenders to a moving target. This drill sharpens your ability to see opportunities and act on them. "Switching play" exercises are equally important. These drills involve moving the ball from one side of the field to the other, quickly and accurately, to exploit space and stretch the opposition. By practicing these switches, you enhance your ability to change the point of attack, making your team more unpredictable. Passing under pressure scenarios are also crucial. Set up drills where you have to make quick passes while being closely marked. This helps you stay composed and accurate even when under duress, a common situation in real matches.

Positioning and awareness are what separate good midfielders from great ones. Always scan the field before receiving the ball. Know where your teammates and opponents are, and plan your next move before the ball arrives. This habit, often referred to as having "eyes in the back of your head," allows you to make quicker, smarter decisions. Finding pockets of space is another critical skill. Drift into open areas where you can receive the ball without immediate pressure. This not only gives you more time on the ball but also disrupts the opponent's defensive shape. Maintaining balance in the midfield is essential. You need to be everywhere but also nowhere in particular—always available for a pass yet never static. Balance your movements to ensure you're supporting both the attack and defense, filling gaps, and maintaining team shape.

Defensive responsibilities are equally important for midfielders. Intercepting passes can turn defense into attack in an instant. Position yourself in passing lanes and anticipate the opponent's moves. Tackling and winning back possession are also crucial duties. When you lose the ball, be the first to press and try to win it back. This relentless effort can disrupt the opponent's rhythm and create opportunities for your team. Supporting the backline is another key responsibility. Drop deep when necessary to provide an extra layer of defense. This not only helps break up the opponent's play but also offers an additional passing option for your defenders, helping them avoid risky clearances.

Let me share an experience that highlights the importance of these skills. During one intense match, our team faced relentless pressure from a highly skilled opponent. Our midfield was the key to absorbing this pressure and turning it into opportunities. One of our midfielders, Adrian, was continuously making himself available for passes. His vision was impeccable; he executed several through balls that split the defense wide open. When we were under pressure, he never panicked. Instead, he used his body to shield the ball, drawing fouls and slowing down the game when needed. Defensively, Adrian was a rock. He intercepted several crucial passes and won back possession numerous times. His balance in the midfield ensured that we were never caught off guard, always maintaining our shape and readiness to counter-attack.

Passing accuracy and vision are not just about technical ability; they involve understanding the game at a deeper level. Practicing drills that simulate real-game scenarios can significantly enhance these skills. For instance, a "through ball" drill where you have to pass between two moving defenders to a forward can replicate the pressure and timing needed in actual matches. "Switching play" exercises, where you quickly move the ball from one side of the field to the other, can help you develop the ability to exploit space and stretch the opposition. Passing under pressure scenarios can be practiced by setting up drills where you have to make quick passes while being closely marked. These drills not only improve your technical skills but also your ability to make quick, smart decisions under pressure.

Positioning and awareness in the midfield are about always being one step ahead. Before you receive the ball, take a quick glance around to see where your teammates and opponents are. This habit allows you to make quicker, smarter decisions. Finding pockets of space is another critical skill. Drift into open areas where you can receive the ball without immediate pressure. This not only gives you more time on the ball but also disrupts the opponent's defensive shape. Maintaining balance in the midfield is essential. You need to be everywhere but also nowhere in particular—always available for a pass yet never static. Balance your movements to ensure you're supporting both the attack and defense, filling gaps, and maintaining team shape.

Another memorable moment involved a midfielder named James, who was known for his exceptional vision and passing accuracy. During a high-stakes game, he executed a perfect "switching play," moving the ball from the crowded left side to the open right flank in one swift motion. This switch caught the opponents off guard, creating a clear path for our winger to advance and cross the ball, leading to a crucial goal. James's ability to scan the field and find that perfect pass was the turning point in the match. It was a clear demonstration of how mastering these skills can make a significant impact on the game.

The balance between offensive and defensive responsibilities, the precision in passing and distribution, the acute awareness of positioning, and the relentless defensive effort are what define a top-class midfielder. By focusing on these areas and continually practicing, you can develop the skills needed to control the midfield, support your team, and influence the outcome of the game.

5.3 Defensive Positioning and Tactics

During my early coaching days, one particular match stood out. Our defense was under relentless pressure, and it was clear that our players needed a better understanding of positioning. Defensive positioning is the backbone of any successful defensive strategy. Staying goal-side of attackers is a fundamental principle. This means positioning yourself between the attacker and the goal, ensuring they have to get past you to score. It sounds simple, but it requires constant vigilance and awareness of both the ball and the opponent. By staying goal-side, you make it harder for attackers to find space and easier for your goalkeeper to anticipate shots.

Maintaining a compact shape is another crucial aspect. When defending, the team should move as a unit, maintaining a tight formation. This reduces gaps and makes it harder for the opposition to penetrate. Imagine a well-organized wall that shifts together based on the ball's position. This compactness forces the attacking team to play around you rather than through you, buying time for your team to regroup and counter-attack. Communication with team-mates is essential here. Constantly talk to each other, calling out positions and movements. This ensures everyone stays on the same page, maintaining the defensive shape and covering any potential gaps.

Tackling is an art that requires impeccable timing. Rushing into a tackle without timing can leave you exposed and the opponent with a clear path to goal. "Timed Tackling" drills are excellent for honing this skill. In these drills, defenders practice timing their tackles to perfection, waiting for the right moment when the attacker is slightly off balance or has taken a heavy touch. Another useful exercise is "Jockeying." This involves guiding the attacker away from dangerous areas without committing to a tackle too early. By staying close and blocking their path, you force mistakes or poor decisions. One-on-one defensive scenarios are also invaluable. These drills simulate real-game situations where you must make split-second decisions on whether to tackle, jockey, or intercept.

Reading the game is what separates the best defenders from the rest. It's not just about physical ability but also about understanding and anticipating the play. Watching the opponent's body language can provide crucial clues. Are they looking to pass, dribble, or shoot? Analyzing the play as it develops helps you anticipate the next move. Is the winger about to cross, or will they cut inside? Positioning to intercept passes is another key skill. Place yourself in passing lanes, making it harder for the opposition to complete their passes. This proactive approach allows you to break up play and launch counter-attacks.

Organizing the defense is a role that often falls to experienced defenders and the goalkeeper. Leading the defensive line involves positioning yourself to see the entire field and directing your teammates accordingly. Use clear, concise commands to ensure everyone knows their role. Communicating with the goalkeeper and other defenders is vital. The goalkeeper has a unique vantage point and can see the entire field. Regularly check in with them to adjust your positioning. Coordinating offside traps is another advanced tactic. By stepping up in unison, you can catch attackers offside, disrupting their play and winning back possession. This requires precise timing and absolute trust in your teammates.

One memorable game highlighted the importance of these defensive principles. We were up against a formidable attacking team, and our defense needed to be flawless. I remember our central defender, Sean, who was exceptional that day. He constantly communicated, ensuring everyone stayed goal-side of their markers. Our defense moved as a unit, maintaining a compact shape that frustrated the opposing attackers. Sean's tackling was impeccable, timing each challenge perfectly. He also read the game brilliantly, intercepting several crucial passes. His leadership in organizing the defense was evident as we successfully executed several offside traps, catching the opponents off guard. Sean's performance was a masterclass in defensive positioning and tactics.

Being a great defender requires a blend of physical skills, mental acuity, and leadership. By focusing on staying goal-side, maintaining a compact shape, and communicating effectively, you can create a formidable defense. Practicing timed tackling, reading the game, and organizing the defensive line further enhances these abilities. These principles and techniques are the foundation of a strong defense, ensuring your team remains resilient and difficult to break down.

5.4 GOALKEEPER TRAINING ESSENTIALS

I remember the first time I stood in a regulation sized goal with a young player. The goal seemed enormous, and the idea of stopping a fast-moving ball felt daunting to both of us. But with the right training, goalkeepers can transform from hesitant to heroes on the pitch. The foundation of any good goalkeeper starts with the basic stance and positioning. The ready position is crucial. Keep your knees slightly bent, weight on the balls of your feet, and hands out and ready. This stance allows for quick lateral movements and ensures you're always prepared to react. Your positioning relative to the ball and goal is equally important. Stay centered in front of the goal, adjusting your stance based on the situation. If the ball is wide, shift your position to cover the near post, always keeping yourself between the ball and the goal. This constant adjustment ensures that you're always in the best position to make a save.

Shot-stopping techniques are the bread and butter of a goalkeeper's skill set. "Diving Saves" drills are essential for improving your ability to stop shots directed at the corners of the goal. Start with a simple drill where you dive to your left and right to stop low shots. As you become more comfortable, introduce high dives, focusing on extending your arms and landing safely. "Reaction Save" exercises can drastically improve your reflexes. Have a coach or teammate shoot from close range with minimal warning, forcing you to react quickly. This sharpens your ability to make split-second decisions. Positioning for different types of shots is another critical aspect. For low shots, get your body low and use your hands to scoop the ball. For high shots, ensure your hands are positioned high and ready to catch or deflect the ball. Practicing these techniques regularly will build the muscle memory needed to react instinctively during games.

Commanding the penalty area is more than just stopping shots; it's about owning your space and instilling confidence in your defense. Coming off the line for crosses is a key skill. When a cross is delivered into the box, step off your line decisively and either catch or punch the ball clear. Hesitation can lead to confusion and missed opportunities for the opposing team. Communication with defenders is another vital element. Constantly talk to your backline, letting them know where attackers are and when you're coming off your line. Clear, loud commands like "keeper's ball" or "man on" can prevent mix-ups and ensure everyone is on the same page. Organizing set-piece defenses is another responsibility. For corners and free-kicks, position your defenders to cover key areas and mark opponents. Direct them to form a wall or cover the posts, ensuring that your goal is well protected from different angles.

Distribution skills are often overlooked but are crucial for starting counterattacks and maintaining possession. Accurate throwing and kicking techniques can turn defense into offense in an instant. When throwing, use an overhand motion for distance and accuracy. Aim for a teammate's feet or chest, making it easier for them to control the ball. For kicks, plant your non-kicking foot beside the ball and strike with your laces for power. Practice "Quick Distribution" drills to enhance these abilities. Set up targets at various distances and challenge yourself to hit them quickly and accurately. Decision-making for starting counterattacks is equally important. Assess the field quickly and decide whether to throw, kick, or roll the ball. If you see a teammate in space, act fast to launch a counterattack. This quick decision-making can catch the opposition off guard and create scoring opportunities for your team.

One of the most memorable moments in my coaching career was watching a young goalkeeper named Donny develop these skills. When he first joined the team, he was hesitant and unsure of his positioning. But through consistent practice of the ready position and shot-stopping drills, his confidence grew. He mastered the art of diving saves, reacting quickly to close-range shots with ease. His ability to command the penalty area became evident during a crucial match. Donny confidently came off his line to punch away a dangerous cross, preventing a sure goal. His communication with the defenders was clear and assertive, organizing them effectively during set-pieces. His distribution skills also improved significantly. He could launch quick counterattacks with precise throws and powerful kicks, turning defense into offense seamlessly.

In soccer, every position is vital, but goalkeepers hold a unique role. Their stance, shot-stopping techniques, command of the penalty area, and distribution skills set them apart. Goal-keeping is not for everyone either. You must have the mindset of winning the ball at any cost, which oftentimes means laying your body on the line and taking a hit. By mastering these essentials, goalkeepers can become the backbone of their team, instilling confidence and providing a solid last line of defense. Donny's journey from a hesitant rookie to a confident, commanding goalkeeper was a testament to the power of dedicated training and practice. His story serves as a reminder that with the right techniques and mindset, any young player can excel in this challenging but rewarding position.

6. Fun and Engaging Drills

One sunny afternoon, I watched the kids as they played a game of "Red Light, Green Light" on the soccer field. Their laughter echoed across the park, and their enthusiasm was infectious. It was a simple game, but it was doing wonders for their coordination and understanding of basic soccer movements. This moment reminded me how essential it is to incorporate fun and engaging drills into our training sessions. These drills not only teach vital soccer skills but also keep the kids excited about coming to practice.

6.1 Game-Based Drills for U6 Players

Exploring movement is a fantastic way to get young players comfortable with their bodies and the ball. One of my favorite drills for this is "Red Light, Green Light." It's straightforward: players dribble the ball and must stop when the coach shouts "red light" and move again when "green light" is called. This game teaches them to control the ball while paying attention to instructions, making it both fun and educational. Another great drill is "Follow the Leader," where kids mimic the coach's movements while dribbling. Whether the coach is weaving through cones or making quick turns, the children learn to keep the ball close and react quickly, enhancing their dribbling skills.

Developing ball control skills through playful activities is crucial at this age. One effective and enjoyable drill is the "Soccer Obstacle Course." Set up cones, tunnels, and small goals for the kids to navigate while dribbling. This course challenges their control and agility, making them more comfortable with the ball at their feet. Another engaging activity is the "Treasure Hunt." Scatter small objects or cones around the field and have the players dribble to collect them. This game disguises learning as fun, encouraging them to focus on their dribbling while aiming to gather as many treasures as possible. These activities not only improve their ball control but also keep them entertained and eager to participate.

Introducing basic team concepts through cooperative games helps young players understand the value of teamwork. "Sharks and Minnows" is a fantastic game for this purpose. In this game, one player acts as the shark, trying to steal the ball from the others, who are the minnows. This drill teaches children to protect the ball and work together to avoid the shark. "Soccer Relay Races" are another excellent team-based activity. Divide the players into teams and set up a relay course where they must dribble the ball to a designated point and pass it to the next teammate. This game fosters a sense of camaraderie and cooperation, as they work together to complete the relay. These team-based drills are not only fun but also instill the importance of working as a unit.

Encouraging creativity with the ball is essential for developing confident and imaginative players. "Freestyle Dribbling" is a perfect drill for this. Give the players time to experiment with different moves and tricks, allowing them to express themselves with the ball. Whether it's trying out a new turn or a fancy footwork move, this drill encourages them to be creative and confident in their abilities. Another fun activity is "Obstacle Creation," where kids design their own dribbling courses using cones. Letting them take charge of the setup fosters creativity and problem-solving skills. They can challenge themselves and their teammates by creating unique and exciting courses. These creative drills not only develop their technical skills but also build their confidence and enjoyment of the game.

Interactive Element: Creativity Corner

Set up a "Creativity Corner" during practice where kids can experiment with different moves and design their own obstacle courses. Encourage them to share their creations with the team and explain the challenges they've set up. This interactive element fosters creativity, teamwork, and leadership skills.

Incorporating these game-based drills into your U6 training sessions will create a dynamic and enjoyable environment for the kids. Exploring movement, developing ball control, introducing team concepts, and encouraging creativity are all essential components of a well-rounded soccer practice. These drills not only teach vital skills but also keep the young players engaged and excited about soccer.

6.2 INTERACTIVE DRILLS FOR U8 TEAMS

One Thursday night, as the sun was setting over the soccer field, I watched the kids eagerly gather for practice. Their energy was contagious, and I knew we needed drills that could both harness their enthusiasm and develop their skills. Incorporating skill-based games was the key. "King of the Ring" quickly became a favorite. In this game, each player tries to keep their ball inside a designated area while attempting to kick others' balls out. It's a fantastic way to teach ball control and spatial awareness. The kids love the competitive element, and it's incredible to see how quickly they learn to protect their ball while strategizing to eliminate others.

"Passing Pairs" is another effective skill-based game. In this drill, players pair up and must complete a set number of passes while moving around the field. This exercise emphasizes the importance of accurate passing and constant movement. It also teaches players to communicate with their partners, making them more cohesive on the field. Watching the pairs work together, calling out to each other, and adjusting their positions is a testament to how interactive drills can enhance both technical skills and teamwork.

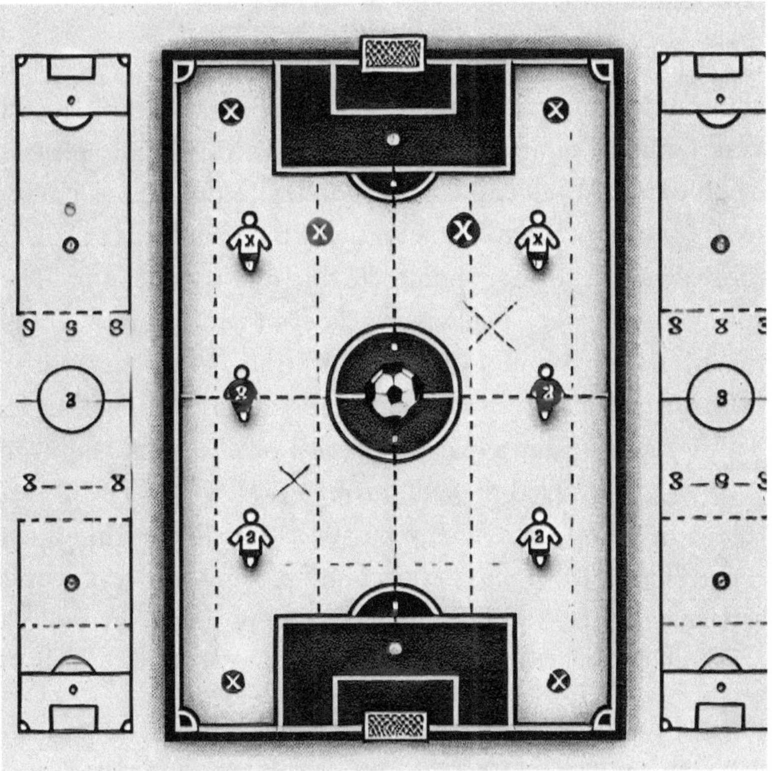

3v3 on a small-sided field

Small-sided games are invaluable for encouraging more touches on the ball and developing teamwork. "3v3 Mini Matches" are perfect for this. These small matches allow each player to be more involved in the game, promoting quick decision-making and constant engagement. With fewer players on the field, each child has more opportunities to pass, dribble, and shoot, which accelerates their development. Another great small-sided game is the "End Zone Game." Instead of scoring in a traditional goal, players score by dribbling or passing into an end zone. This variation encourages them to focus on ball control and strategic passing, rather than just aiming for the goal. It also adds a new layer of excitement and challenge to the game.

Creating interactive challenges that require teamwork and communication can transform a practice session. "Tug of War Dribble" is a fantastic example. In this game, players dribble towards a central point and try to pull the ball away from their opponent. It's a great way to teach them to shield the ball and use their bodies to maintain possession. The competitive nature of the game keeps them engaged, while the need for communication and strategy enhances their teamwork skills. Another engaging drill is "Passing Gates." Set up multiple gates (pairs of cones) on the field, and have pairs or groups pass the ball through these gates. The objective is to complete as many passes as possible within a set time. This drill emphasizes accurate passing and teamwork, as players need to communicate and position themselves effectively to succeed.

Incorporating technology into drills can make them even more engaging. "Interactive Cone Drills" are a fantastic way to use simple technology. Cones that light up or make sounds can guide players through various drills, adding an element of surprise and excitement. For example, set up cones that light up in different colors, and have players dribble to the corresponding cone as it lights up. This drill sharpens their reaction time and keeps them on their toes. "App-Based Challenges" are another innovative approach. Utilize soccer training apps that provide interactive drills and track progress. These apps can set challenges, like completing a certain number of passes or dribbles within a time limit. The kids can see their progress in real-time, which keeps them motivated and eager to improve.

One practice session, we used an app that set up a "Passing Challenge." The app tracked the number of successful passes each pair completed within a set time. The kids were thrilled to see their scores and were motivated to beat their previous records. It added a competitive edge to the practice and made the drill more engaging. The combination of skill-based games, small-sided matches, interactive challenges, and technology created a dynamic and exciting training environment. The kids were not only improving their skills but also having a blast, which is the ultimate goal.

6.3 Competitive Drills for U10 Teams

One sunny morning, I saw the kids eagerly lining up for a speed dribble race. Their faces were a mix of determination and excitement. Creating drills that develop speed and agility in a competitive environment is key for U10 players. Speed dribble races are an excellent way to combine these elements. Set up a series of cones and have the players dribble through them as quickly as possible, racing against each other. This not only improves their dribbling skills but also their speed and coordination. Ladder drills are another fantastic tool. Using an agility ladder, players navigate through it, focusing on quick footwork and precise movements. These drills are not only fun but also incredibly effective in enhancing their agility and speed on the field.

One-on-one challenges add a thrilling element to practice, pushing players to use their skills in competitive scenarios. The "1v1 Attacking and Defending" drill is a favorite among the kids. Players take turns trying to dribble past each other to score. This drill sharpens their attacking moves and defensive skills. Mirror dribbling is another engaging exercise. In this drill, one player leads while the other tries to mimic their movements. It's like a game of follow-the-leader but with a competitive twist. This drill helps improve dribbling control and responsiveness, making players more adept at handling one-on-one situations in games.

Organizing team-based competitions builds camaraderie and competitive spirit. Capture the Flag Soccer is an exciting game where teams compete to capture a flag while dribbling and passing. It combines elements of strategy, teamwork, and technical skills. Players must work together to protect their flag while trying to steal the opponent's. This game fosters a sense of unity and collaboration. Another engaging activity is tournament-style matches. Set up mini-tournaments with quick games, allowing players to experience the thrill of competition in a structured format. These matches give them a taste of real-game scenarios, helping them understand the dynamics of team play and competition. The excitement of a tournament atmosphere keeps them motivated and eager to participate.

Ladder drill for u10

Allowing players to showcase their skills in a competitive setting is both rewarding and motivating. Skills challenges are a fantastic way to do this. Set up competitions where players compete in dribbling, passing, and shooting challenges. For example, create a dribbling course with cones and time each player as they navigate through it. Award points for accuracy and speed. Passing challenges can involve hitting specific targets or completing a set number of passes within a time limit. Shooting challenges can focus on accuracy and power, with players aiming for targets in the goal. These challenges not only improve their skills but also give them a sense of accomplishment as they see their progress.

Freestyle contests are another fun and engaging way to let players showcase their skills. In these contests, players perform their best moves, judged by peers or coaches. Whether it's a fancy dribble, a creative pass, or a powerful shot, freestyle contests encourage creativity and confidence. We would set up an "Americas Got Soccer Talent" competition at the end of the year and invite the parents to come and participate as judges. Watching their teammates showcase their unique skills can inspire others to try new things and push their boundaries. It's a fantastic way to build a positive and supportive team environment where everyone celebrates each other's achievements.

One memorable practice session involved a combination of these drills. We started with speed dribble races and ladder drills to warm up. The kids were buzzing with energy; their competitive spirits ignited. We then moved on to 1v1 attacking and defending, followed by a thrilling game of Capture the Flag Soccer. The highlight was the skills challenge, where each player got a chance to showcase their dribbling, passing, and shooting skills. The excitement and camaraderie were palpable. The kids were not only improving their skills but also having a blast, which is the ultimate goal of these competitive drills.

6.4 Incorporating Mini-Games into Practice

One of the most effective ways to keep young players engaged and motivated is by incorporating mini-games into practice sessions. These games provide numerous benefits, starting with the increased touches on the ball. In a full-sized game, a single player might only touch the ball a handful of times. Mini-games, with fewer players and a smaller area, ensure that everyone gets more opportunities to interact with the ball. This frequent contact helps develop their skills more rapidly. Additionally, mini-games enhance decision-making by placing players in various scenarios where they must think quickly and react accordingly. These games disguise conditioning as fun, improving fitness levels without the monotony of traditional drills.

Designing effective mini-games requires clear objectives and rules. Each game should have a specific focus, whether it's dribbling, passing, or shooting. Clear rules ensure that everyone understands how to play and what is expected of them. Balanced teams are crucial to maintaining competitiveness and ensuring that all players are equally challenged. This balance keeps the game engaging for everyone involved. Mini-games should incorporate various skills within the game to provide a well-rounded practice. For example, a game might require players to dribble, pass, and shoot, offering a comprehensive skill workout in a fun, competitive setting.

One of my favorite mini-games is a variation of tag that incorporates dribbling and passing. In this game, players must dribble the ball while trying to tag their opponents with it. It sharpens their dribbling skills and forces them to keep their heads up. Another engaging mini-game is "Cone Knockdown." Set up cones as targets and have players try to knock them down by passing the ball. This game improves passing accuracy and adds an element of competition. Both games are simple yet effective, keeping the players engaged while honing their skills.

Adapting mini-games to suit different skill levels and objectives can make them even more effective. Modifying the field size is one way to adjust the difficulty. A smaller field makes the game more challenging by reducing the space available, while a larger field has the opposite effect. Adjusting the number of players also changes the dynamics. Fewer players mean more touches and decisions for each child, while more players increase the complexity of the game. Adding or changing game rules can focus the practice on specific skills. For instance, you might require that all passes be made with the weaker foot or that players must make a certain number of passes before they can score.

These adjustments keep the games fresh and challenging, ensuring that players continue to develop their skills. It is also helpful to introduce a "neutral" player who plays offense for either team when they have possession. This changes the dynamic when the offense has the ball since they are a man up in the attack. Rotating your midfielders as the "neutral" player is beneficial since they are usually the ones connecting passes, but it can help any player develop transition play and quick decision making.

I remember a session where we adapted a simple game of tag to focus on passing. We divided the players into pairs and scattered cones around the field. The objective was to pass the ball and tag the cones, earning points for each successful tag. As the game progressed, we modified the rules to require weaker foot passes and increased the number of cones. The players were fully engaged, and their passing accuracy improved noticeably. This adaptability makes mini-games an invaluable tool in any coach's arsenal.

Cone Knockout Game

Another memorable practice involved a game of "Cone Knockdown." We set up two teams, each with a row of cones to defend. The goal was to knock down the opponent's cones while protecting their own. The kids quickly grasped the competitive aspect sond were fully invested in the game. As the session progressed, we adjusted the field size and added rules to increase the difficulty. The players were not only exhausted by the end of the drill but also more skilled and confident in their passing abilities. The excitement and energy they brought to the game were palpable, underscoring the effectiveness of mini-games in creating an engaging and productive practice environment.

6.5 DRILLS FOR IMPROVING TEAMWORK

One of the most memorable moments in my coaching experience was watching a group of young players work together seamlessly, each understanding their role and supporting their teammates. This cohesion didn't happen overnight; it was built through carefully designed drills that emphasize teamwork. One such drill is "Linked Dribbling." Here, players dribble while holding hands or connecting with a string. This simple connection forces them to communicate and coordinate their movements, reinforcing the importance of working together. It's a fun way to teach them that success on the field often depends on how well they can function as a unit.

"Group Passing Challenges" are another effective way to foster teamwork. In this drill, teams must complete a passing sequence using their hands at first without dropping the ball. Set up a series of cones to create a path and have the players pass the ball through each checkpoint. This exercise requires precise passing and constant communication. If the ball drops, they have to start over, which adds a layer of challenge and encourages them to focus. This drill not only improves their passing skills but also teaches them to rely on their teammates and work towards a common goal. After a few attempts, the ball should be placed back on the ground and the drill should be run using their feet. The transition should show them that they need to be as comfortable with a ball at their feet as they are running with it in their hands and eventually better.

Creating activities that emphasize communication on the field is crucial for developing team cohesion. "Silent Soccer" is a unique and engaging drill where players must complete tasks without speaking, relying solely on non-verbal cues. This activity sharpens their ability to read body language and make quick decisions based on their teammates' movements. Another engaging exercise is "Call and Response Drills." In these drills, players call out their names before receiving a pass. This ensures that everyone is paying attention and ready to react. It also instills the habit of constant communication, which is vital during games.

Trust-building exercises can significantly enhance team dynamics. "Trust Dribble" is a drill where one player is blindfolded and guided by a teammate through a dribbling course. The guiding player must use verbal instructions to help their partner navigate the obstacles. This exercise builds trust and reinforces the idea that teammates need to rely on each other. "Buddy Runs" are another excellent trust-building activity. In this drill, pairs work together to complete running and dribbling challenges. Each player must depend on their partner to achieve success, fostering a sense of mutual support and cooperation.

Team strategy drills help players understand and execute team strategies effectively. "Tactical Mini-Games" are small-sided games with specific tactical objectives, such as maintaining possession or executing a high press. These games simulate real match conditions and teach players how to implement team strategies in a competitive environment. "Role-Specific Drills" are another valuable tool. These activities focus on understanding and performing specific roles within the team structure. For example, defenders might work on positioning and marking, while forwards practice making runs and finishing. These drills ensure that each player understands their responsibilities and how they contribute to the team's overall strategy.

One practice session stands out where we focused on "Linked Dribbling" and **"Silent Soccer."** The kids were initially hesitant about holding hands while dribbling, but they quickly adapted. It was fascinating to see them develop a rhythm and communicate through subtle cues. When we moved on to "Silent Soccer," the transformation was incredible. The field was filled with focused, attentive players making eye contact and reading each other's movements. These drills not only improved their technical skills but also brought them closer as a team.

Another memorable day involved "Trust Dribble" and "Buddy Runs." Watching the blindfolded players navigate the course with their teammates' guidance was heartwarming. The trust and communication they displayed were remarkable. In the "Buddy Runs," pairs encouraged and supported each other through each challenge, building a strong sense of camaraderie. These exercises showed that building trust and communication off the ball is just as important as technical skills.

Incorporating these drills into your training sessions will not only improve your players' technical abilities but also foster a strong sense of teamwork and trust. Cooperative drills, communication-focused activities, trust-building exercises, and team strategy drills are all essential for developing a cohesive and effective team. By focusing on these areas, you can create an environment where players support and rely on each other, both on and off the field.

As we wrap up this chapter, remember that teamwork is at the heart of soccer. Building these skills early on lays the foundation for future success. In the next chapter, we'll explore the importance of family involvement in youth soccer and how it can enhance the overall experience for young players.

THE SOCCER SUCCESS PLAYBOOK
A STEP-BY-STEP GUIDE FOR NEW COACHES
AND PARENTS THROUGH THE YOUTH SOCCER
LANDSCAPE. EARLY DEVELOPMENT AGES
EDITION.

"The beautiful game is not just about playing. It's about learning, growing, and becoming a better person both on and off the field."

— *ANONYMOUS*

People who share their knowledge and passion make the world a brighter place. So, let's spread the love for soccer and help others!

Would you help a new soccer parent or coach—someone eager to support young players but unsure where to begin?

My goal is to make youth soccer easy to understand, enjoyable, and accessible for everyone.

But I need your help to reach more parents and coaches who could use this guidance.

Most people pick books based on reviews, so your thoughts could make a huge difference for someone searching for help in navigating youth soccer.

It costs nothing, takes just a minute, and could completely change someone's soccer journey. Your review could help...

...one more parent confidently support their child on the field

....one more coach create a positive, fun experience for the team

....one more young player find their passion and shine brightly

....one more family share unforgettable moments together.

To lend a hand, just click the link below and leave a review:

Leave a review on Amazon!

If you believe in encouraging others and creating positive experiences for young players, you're my kind of person. Thank you so much for making a difference!

Warm regards,

Matthew Eric

7. Inspirational Stories and Role Models

When I think back to my early days as a soccer coach, I remember an evening practice that stood out. The sun was setting, casting a golden hue over the field, and a young player named Marcos was struggling with his confidence. He had immense potential but was weighed down by self-doubt. I decided to share some stories of famous soccer prodigies, hoping to inspire him. As I recounted the journeys of these remarkable athletes, I saw a spark in Marco's eyes. He realized that even the greatest players had faced obstacles and had to work hard to achieve their dreams. This chapter is dedicated to those stories, which I hope will inspire you as much as they did Marcos.

7.1 SUCCESS STORIES OF YOUNG SOCCER PRODIGIES

Lionel Messi, often hailed as one of the greatest soccer players of all time, had a challenging start. Born in Rosario, Argentina, Messi was diagnosed with growth hormone deficiency at a young age. This condition meant that his body couldn't produce enough growth hormone, severely affecting his growth and development. His family faced significant financial hardships, struggling to afford the expensive hormone treatments that Messi needed. Yet, his passion for soccer never wavered. Every day, he received hormone injections and continued to play the sport he loved. Messi's early life was a testament to his determination and resilience. His family eventually moved to Spain, where he joined FC Barcelona's youth academy, La Masia. This move was a turning point in his career, allowing him access to world-class training facilities and mentorship from experienced coaches. It should also be noted that Messi was denied attendance to many academies before Carles Rexach, FC Barcelona's sporting director, agreed to sign his contract on a napkin, making the deal permanent. Everyone thought he was too small and undersized to compete at a pro level. Now he has won the World Cup, two Copa Americas, ten La Liga titles, four UEFA Champions League titles, three UEFA Super Cups, three FIFA Club World Cups, and the Ballon d'Or, which is awarded to the "world's best player" eight times. Size was never a limitation for Messi and serves as a great lesson to all future players.

Christian Pulisic's journey through the youth leagues in the United States is another inspiring tale. Growing up in Hershey, Pennsylvania, Pulisic showed an early talent for soccer. However, the path to professional soccer in the U.S. was not as well-paved as it is in Europe. Although we will delve more into the political and economic landscape of youth soccer in the US in our next book, for now it is safe to say that Pulisic's family made significant sacrifices to support his dreams. They navigated the complexities of youth soccer leagues, often traveling long distances for games and training sessions. Despite the lack of access to top-tier training facilities, Pulisic's dedication to his craft was unwavering.

His big break came when he joined the U.S. Soccer Development Academy, which provided him with better training opportunities and exposure to scouts. His hard work and perseverance paid off when he was signed by Borussia Dortmund in Germany, making him one of the youngest American players to join a top European club.

Marta, often referred to as the "Queen of Soccer," had humble beginnings in Brazil. Growing up in a small town with limited resources, Marta's love for soccer was evident from a young age. She often played barefoot with boys in the streets, using makeshift balls made of socks and plastic bags. The lack of formal training facilities didn't deter her. Instead, it fueled her determination to succeed. Marta's talent caught the eye of a local coach, who introduced her to a youth academy. Despite the financial challenges and societal barriers she faced as a female soccer player, Marta's skills shone brightly. Her dedication to the sport, combined with the mentorship she received, helped her rise through the ranks. She eventually joined the Brazilian national team, becoming one of the most celebrated female soccer players in history. She has played in six FIFA Women's World Cups from 2003-2023 and holds the record for most World Cup goals scored across both men's and women's tournaments.

Overcoming obstacles is a common thread in the stories of these young prodigies. Financial hardships, lack of access to quality training facilities, and the challenge of balancing education with soccer were hurdles they had to navigate. Messi's family struggled to afford his medical treatments, but their sacrifice paid off when he joined Barcelona. Pulisic's family faced the logistical challenges of navigating the U.S. youth soccer system, but their perseverance led him to Europe. Marta's journey was marked by societal barriers and financial constraints, yet her talent and determination propelled her to international stardom.

Training and development played a crucial role in their success. These prodigies dedicated countless hours to individual skill drills, honing their abilities through repetitive practice. Messi's time at La Masia was characterized by rigorous training routines and a focus on technical skills. Pulisic's development in the U.S. Soccer Development Academy involved intense training sessions and exposure to high-level competition. Marta's journey through local youth academies in Brazil provided her with the foundational skills and mentorship needed to excel. The guidance from experienced coaches and mentors was instrumental in shaping their careers, providing them with the knowledge and support needed to reach their full potential. None of them could have achieved these levels of success on their own and that message is extremely important to relay to the youth.

The achievements and milestones these young players reached early in their careers are nothing short of remarkable. Messi won numerous youth championships with Barcelona, breaking records at a young age and making his debut for the senior team as a teenager. Pulisic's journey saw him representing the U.S. national team as a teenager, becoming one of the youngest players to score in World Cup qualifiers. His performances in Europe have solidified his status as one of the top American soccer players. Marta's achievements include winning multiple FIFA World Player of the Year awards and representing Brazil in several World Cups and Olympic Games. Her impact on women's soccer is profound, inspiring countless young girls to pursue their dreams.

These stories highlight the importance of hard work, dedication, and resilience in achieving success. Whether you're an aspiring player, a supportive parent, or a dedicated coach, the journeys of Messi, Pulisic, and Marta serve as powerful reminders that with determination and perseverance, anything is possible. Their early struggles, rigorous training routines, and significant achievements underscore the value of dedication and the transformative power of soccer.

7.2 FEMALE SOCCER STARS: OVERCOMING CHALLENGES

Megan Rapinoe stands as a beacon of resilience and advocacy in the soccer world. She's not just known for her skill on the field but also for her relentless fight for equal pay. Rapinoe, co-captain of the U.S. Women's National Team, made headlines by leading a lawsuit against the U.S. Soccer Federation over pay discrimination. Her bold stance highlighted a glaring inequality: the women's team, despite their success, earned significantly less than their male counterparts. Rapinoe's advocacy didn't stop at pay equity; she was also an early supporter of the Black Lives Matter movement, taking a knee during the national anthem in solidarity with Colin Kaepernick. Her actions, though met with resistance, underscored her commitment to justice and equality in sports.

Abby Wambach, another iconic figure, has been a tireless advocate for gender equality in sports. With a fierce determination, Wambach used her platform to speak out against the disparities female athletes face. She pushed for better training facilities, more media coverage, and greater financial support for women in sports. Wambach's battle wasn't just with external forces; she also faced personal challenges. Balancing her role as a professional athlete with her personal life was no small feat. Yet, she managed to excel on the field, becoming one of the most prolific goal scorers in soccer history. Wambach's legacy is not just her goals but her unwavering commitment to leveling the playing field for future generations of female athletes.

These female athletes didn't just face external challenges; their journeys were marked by limited resources and societal expectations. In many cases, they had to fight for access to training facilities and resources that were readily available to their male counterparts. Rapinoe, Wambach, and Marta all encountered situations where they had to prove their worth repeatedly. They had to balance their professional careers with personal lives, navigating the complexities of being female athletes in a male-dominated sport. Their stories are not just about overcoming barriers but about redefining what it means to be a successful athlete.

The achievements and recognition these female soccer stars have garnered are nothing short of phenomenal. **Alex Morgan's** World Cup victories with the U.S. Women's National Team are a testament to her skill, determination, and leadership. Morgan has been a vital part of the team's success, her goals and assists have been crucial in their triumphs. Off the field, she has become a role model, advocating for gender equality and inspiring young girls to pursue their dreams. **Hope Solo**, with her record-breaking goalkeeping performances, has set new standards in women's soccer. Solo's agility, sharp reflexes, and commanding presence in goal have earned her numerous awards and recognition as one of the best goalkeepers in the world. **Mia Hamm's** influence on women's soccer globally cannot be overstated. As one of the pioneers of the sport, Hamm's achievements paved the way for future generations. Her skill, sportsmanship, and dedication to the game have left an indelible mark on soccer, inspiring countless young players to follow in her footsteps.

These female athletes have not only excelled in their careers but have also become role models and mentors for the next generation. Through community outreach programs, they have engaged with young players, sharing their experiences and offering guidance. Rapinoe's involvement in various community initiatives, including advocating for LGBTQ+ rights and social justice, has made her a powerful role model. Wambach's coaching and mentoring of young female players have provided invaluable support and encouragement, helping them navigate the challenges of professional sports. Marta's advocacy for women's rights in sports has inspired many young girls in Brazil and beyond to pursue soccer, showing them that their dreams are valid and achievable.

Their influence extends beyond the soccer field. By advocating for women's rights and equality, these athletes have contributed to broader societal changes. Their efforts in promoting gender equality in sports have led to increased visibility and support for female athletes, encouraging more girls to take up soccer and other sports. Through their dedication and advocacy, Rapinoe, Wambach, and Marta have not only changed the landscape of women's soccer but have also inspired a new generation to dream big and fight for their rights.

As you read these stories, remember that the path to success is rarely smooth. These female soccer stars faced numerous challenges but overcame them through hard work, determination, and a belief in their abilities. Their journeys serve as powerful reminders that with resilience and perseverance, you too can achieve greatness in whatever field you choose.

7.3 LESSONS FROM PROFESSIONAL COACHES

When I think of the profound impact a coach can have on a player, I often reflect on the philosophies of some of the greatest minds in soccer. Take **Pep Guardiola**, for instance. His approach to coaching is centered around possession and team cohesion. Guardiola believes that controlling the ball means controlling the game. His teams, whether it's Barcelona, Bayern Munich, or Manchester City, are known for their quick, precise passing and fluid movement. This style of play not only confuses opponents but also builds a strong sense of unity among players. Guardiola's emphasis on technical ability ensures that every player, from defenders to forwards, can handle the ball with confidence. This philosophy has contributed significantly to the development of players, making them versatile and adaptable. Johan Cruyff is considered the creator of the "Tiki Taka" style of play which is often associated with Spanish football, particularly FC Barcelona and the Spanish national team during the late 2000s and early 2010s. That style was later studied and refined by Pep and gained international acclaim when Spain won the 2010 FIFA World Cup and two consecutive European Championships (2008 and 2012) using this system. Dubbed "Death by Passing," everyone all over the world tried to copy and emulate this style of play from the pro's down to the youth levels. You can still see the concept today in Manchester City, although it has again been refined by Pep because of his players. Another testament to one of the greatest soccer minds in a generation.

Jurgen Klopp, on the other hand, brings a different energy to the field. His high-intensity pressing game, often referred to as "gegenpressing," focuses on winning the ball back as quickly as possible after losing it. Klopp's teams, like Borussia Dortmund and Liverpool, are known for their relentless pursuit of the ball, putting immense pressure on opponents. This approach requires exceptional fitness and mental toughness, qualities that Klopp instills in his players. His philosophy is not just about physical exertion but also about creating a cohesive unit that works together seamlessly. By fostering a sense of camaraderie and collective effort, Klopp has developed players who are not only skilled but also resilient and determined.

Jill Ellis, the former coach of the U.S. Women's National Team, brings another perspective with her focus on versatility and adaptability. Ellis believes that players should be able to perform in multiple positions and adapt to different tactical setups. This approach was evident in the U.S. team's success in the 2015 and 2019 World Cups, where she constantly adjusted her tactics based on the opponents. Her philosophy encourages players to expand their skill sets and understand the game from various angles. This versatility not only makes players more valuable to their teams but also enhances their overall understanding of the game.

Mentorship and guidance play a crucial role in the development of players under these renowned coaches. One-on-one mentoring sessions are a staple in their approach. Guardiola, for example, often holds individual meetings with his players, discussing their performances, strengths, and areas for improvement. This personalized attention helps players understand their roles better and boosts their confidence. Constructive feedback is another key element. Klopp was known for his honest yet supportive feedback, which helps players recognize their potential and work on their weaknesses. Setting individual and team goals is also vital. Ellis often set specific targets for her players, both short-term and long-term, helping them stay focused and motivated. These goals create a roadmap for players, guiding them through their development journey and ensuring continuous improvement.

Training techniques used by these coaches are innovative and tailored to enhance both individual and team performance. Tactical drills are a cornerstone of their training sessions. Guardiola's sessions often include drills that mimic real-game scenarios, helping players understand positioning, movement, and decision-making. These drills are designed to improve game understanding and develop a player's tactical intelligence. Fitness regimes are also meticulously planned. Klopp's fitness programs are tailored to meet the high demands of his pressing game. These regimes focus on building endurance, strength, and speed, ensuring that players can maintain their intensity throughout the match. Inspirational stories and quotes from professional coaches can also provide valuable insights and motivation. **Sir Alex Ferguson**, the legendary manager of Manchester United, often spoke about leadership and resilience. One of his famous quotes, "Attack wins you games, defense wins you titles," emphasizes the importance of a balanced approach. Ferguson's leadership style, which combined strict discipline with genuine care for his players, has inspired many. **Carlo Ancelotti's** stories of overcoming challenges are equally motivating. Ancelotti, who has managed top clubs like AC Milan, Chelsea, and Real Madrid, often shares anecdotes about dealing with pressure and setbacks. His calm demeanor and strategic thinking have helped his teams navigate difficult situations. **Phil Neville**, the former coach of the England Women's National Team, is known for his motivational speeches. He often emphasized the importance of believing in oneself and the power of teamwork. Neville's ability to uplift his team through words and actions has made a significant impact on his players.

One particular story that stands out is from Ancelotti's time at AC Milan. During the 2005 UEFA Champions League final, Milan faced Liverpool. Despite leading 3-0 at halftime, Milan ended up losing in a dramatic penalty shootout. Ancelotti's response to this heartbreaking defeat was remarkable. Instead of blaming his players, he focused on the positives and used this experience as a learning opportunity. His resilience and calmness in the face of adversity taught his players the importance of staying composed and learning from their mistakes. This approach not only helped Milan bounce back but also strengthened the bond between the coach and his players.

These lessons from professional coaches offer invaluable insights into player development and team dynamics. Their philosophies, mentorship, training techniques, and inspirational stories provide a holistic understanding of what it takes to succeed in soccer. By embracing these lessons, you can enhance your coaching approach, inspire your players, and create a positive and effective training environment.

7.4 INSPIRATIONAL QUOTES TO MOTIVATE PLAYERS

I remember one particular evening practice when the team seemed tired and disheartened. We had lost a few games in a row, and the kids were feeling the weight of those losses. To lift their spirits, I decided to share some inspirational quotes from legendary soccer players. These quotes have a way of resonating deeply, offering wisdom and motivation that can reignite a player's passion for the game. As I gathered the team, I started with a quote from **Ronaldinho**: "I learned all about life with a ball at my feet." The simplicity and depth of his words struck a chord with myself, and I needed to pass that impact on to the kids. They realized that soccer is more than just a game; it's a teacher of life lessons, resilience, and joy.

Next, I shared **Lionel Messi's** powerful words: "You have to fight to reach your dream. You have to sacrifice and work hard for it." Messi's journey from a small boy with a growth hormone deficiency to one of the greatest players in the world is a testament to his relentless dedication. The kids could see that even someone as talented as Messi had to make sacrifices and put in the hard work to achieve his dreams. This quote reminded them that their own struggles and efforts were part of a larger process of growth and achievement.

Pelé's quote, "Success is no accident. It is hard work, perseverance, learning, studying, sacrifice, and most of all, love of what you are doing or learning to do," further emphasized this point. Pelé's words encapsulate the essence of success in any field. The kids understood that their passion for soccer, combined with their willingness to work hard and persevere, would pave the way for their success. These quotes from soccer legends provided them with a renewed sense of purpose and motivation. The perseverance it took for Pele to overcome his life tribulations of poverty, lack of resources, and other obstacles redefined the power of mental toughness and the sheer will to succeed.

An innovative exercise that I instilled with my young teams was challenging them to create their own motivational quote, slogan, or writing sample. Once completed, I had them print it out and hang it in their room where it could be visibly seen. Based on my inspiration from Pele as a young child, I created the following poem as an example to present to my young players.

A Grapefruit Had Fallen

Once upon a time in a village not far

A young boy was born, to be destined a star

He was born to the slums

Lived with the bums

But was never too far from the beating of drums.

The stadium roared

The crowds continuously cried

But he was always too poor to get a ticket inside

His only way in was to play in a game

To become a national legend

As they go chanting his name.

His family was poor and could not buy him a ball

But this could not stop his desire at all

He searched through the streets

Until he finally found

A Grapefruit had fallen

From a tree to the ground.

He started to practice. He started to train.

He played in the heat, the sleet, and the rain.

He juggled his grapefruit from his foot to his head

He would hold it so tight while he slept in his bed.

He would dribble through alleys and kick off the walls

You could hear it come rolling down those nasty old halls

It's what made him a legend the people would say

A sixteen year old boy by the name of Pele'.

He had the strength of an ox

The heart of a lion,

With a vertical leap to the top

Of Mount Zion,

He won the World Cup for a total of three

He did it himself for the whole world to see

Now he sits in his stadium with fortune and fame

His country, the world, chanting his name,

Edson Arantes do Nascmiento

Was never the same.

Teamwork and unity are the cornerstones of soccer. To highlight their importance, I shared some quotes that emphasize these values. **Vince Lombardi's** words, "Individual commitment to a group effort – that is what makes a team work, a company work, a society work, a civilization work," underscore the significance of each player's contribution to the team's success. The kids realized that their individual efforts, when combined, created a powerful force.

Phil Jackson's quote, "The strength of the team is each individual member. The strength of each member is the team," reinforced this idea. It reminded them that their personal growth and contributions made the team stronger. These quotes helped the kids see the value of working together, supporting each other, and striving for collective success.

Overcoming adversity is a theme that resonates with everyone, especially young athletes facing challenges. I shared **Michael Jordan's** profound words: "I've failed over and over and over again in my life. And that is why I succeed." Jordan's acknowledgment of failure as a stepping stone to success was eye-opening for the kids. They realized that setbacks and mistakes were not the end but opportunities to learn and grow. **Les Brown's** quote, "The harder the battle, the sweeter the victory," further emphasized this point. It highlighted the idea that the struggles and challenges they faced would make their successes even more meaningful. These quotes inspired the kids to embrace adversity and use it as fuel for their journey forward.

Motivational quotes from renowned coaches also have a powerful impact. **Ernie Banks** once said, "The only way to prove that you're a good sport is to lose." This quote reminded the kids that sportsmanship is about handling both wins and losses with grace. It encouraged them to view losses as part of the game and to use them as opportunities to improve. **Pelé's** words, "The more difficult the victory, the greater the happiness in winning," resonated deeply. It emphasized that the challenges they faced and overcame would make their victories all the more satisfying. These quotes from coaches and icons provided valuable lessons in sportsmanship, resilience, and the true spirit of competition.

As I looked around at the kids, I could see the change in their expressions. The quotes had reignited their passion and determination. They understood that soccer, like life, is filled with challenges, but with hard work, perseverance, and teamwork, they could overcome any obstacle. These quotes served as a reminder that they were not alone in their struggles and that even the greatest players and coaches faced similar challenges. The kids left practice that evening with a renewed sense of purpose, ready to tackle their next game with confidence.

In the next chapter, we will explore the importance of family involvement in soccer. From cheering on the sidelines to practicing together at home, we'll discuss how families can support their young athletes and create a positive soccer experience.

8. FAMILY INVOLVEMENT IN SOCCER

One sunny afternoon, I had the pleasure of witnessing a family soccer day that transformed our local park into a vibrant hub of activity. Parents, kids, and even grandparents gathered on the grassy field, all eager to participate. The laughter and cheers were infectious. It was clear that soccer had brought this community closer together, turning a simple game into a family affair. This experience underscored the importance of family involvement in youth soccer, not just for the kids but for everyone involved.

8.1 ENCOURAGING FAMILY PARTICIPATION IN SOCCER

Organizing family soccer days can be a fantastic way to foster a love for the game and strengthen family bonds. Picture this: setting up mini-matches in your backyard or a local park where everyone, regardless of age or skill level, can join in. Imagine the thrill of creating mixed-age teams, ensuring that both kids and adults can participate equally. These matches aren't about competition; they're about having fun and enjoying each other's company. You can take it a step further by planning a family soccer tournament. Create team names, make a bracket, and even have small prizes for the winners. It's an excellent way to bring everyone together, creating memories that will last a lifetime.

Family presence and support during games can make a significant difference in a child's experience. Positive cheering and encouragement from the sidelines can boost a young player's confidence and motivation. Bring signs and banners to support the team, making the atmosphere festive and exciting. Celebrate both effort and success—not just the goals scored but the determination and teamwork displayed. Your presence and support show your child that you're invested in their journey, making them feel valued and motivated to keep trying. Remember, it's not just about winning; it's about being there, showing up, and cheering them on every step of the way.

Involving siblings in the soccer journey can create a supportive and inclusive environment. Younger or older siblings can act as assistant coaches or team mascots, giving them a sense of responsibility and involvement. You can create sibling-specific roles, such as water carriers or cheerleaders, making them feel like an essential part of the team. Encouraging siblings to play together at home can foster a sense of camaraderie and healthy competition. These interactions not only strengthen sibling bonds but also teach valuable lessons about teamwork and support.

Family fitness routines that include soccer-based exercises can be a fantastic way to promote health and bonding. Imagine starting your day with a family jog or bike ride to build endurance together. These activities not only improve physical fitness but also create opportunities for meaningful conversations and shared experiences. Group stretching sessions before and after practice can become a family ritual, promoting flexibility and preventing injuries. You can also incorporate family soccer drills and challenges. Set up cones in the backyard and practice dribbling, passing, and shooting together. These activities make exercise fun and engaging, turning fitness into a family affair.

To make family fitness routines more engaging, you can introduce a fun element by organizing family fitness challenges. For instance, you can set weekly goals for the number of laps run or the number of passes completed. Celebrate these milestones with a small reward or a special family activity. This not only keeps everyone motivated but also fosters a sense of achievement and togetherness. Additionally, incorporating soccer-based games like "Red Light, Green Light" or "Sharks and Minnows" into your fitness routine can make the experience enjoyable for everyone, regardless of their age or fitness level.

One memorable family soccer day involved setting up a mini-tournament with mixed-age teams. We created team names, made colorful banners, and even had a scoreboard. The kids loved playing alongside their parents and siblings, and the friendly competition brought out the best in everyone. The highlight of the day was a final match where the youngest players took center stage, cheered on by their families. The joy and excitement on their faces were priceless. It was a perfect example of how family involvement can transform a simple game into a cherished family memory.

Another moment that stands out is when a group of parents decided to create a "cheer squad" for their kids' team. They brought homemade signs, pom-poms, and even choreographed a simple cheer. The kids were thrilled to see their parents so actively involved and supportive. It boosted their confidence and made them feel like superstars. The positive energy from the sidelines was infectious, creating a supportive and encouraging atmosphere that benefited everyone on the field.

Involving siblings can also create memorable experiences. I recall a practice where an older sibling took on the role of assistant coach. He helped set up drills, offered encouragement, and even demonstrated some skills. The younger players looked up to him, and his involvement added a new dimension to the practice. It not only helped the younger players improve but also gave the older sibling a sense of responsibility and pride. These interactions can strengthen family bonds and create a supportive environment for everyone involved.

Family fitness routines can be a great way to bond and stay healthy together. I remember a family who started a tradition of going for a jog every Saturday morning before soccer practice. They would run through the neighborhood, chatting and laughing along the way. After the jog, they would spend a few minutes stretching together and discussing their plans for the day. This routine not only improved their fitness but also brought them closer as a family. They looked forward to these Saturday mornings, and it became a cherished family tradition.

By encouraging family participation in soccer, you can create a supportive and inclusive environment that benefits everyone involved. Organizing family soccer days, cheering from the sidelines, involving siblings, and introducing family fitness routines can enhance the soccer experience and strengthen family bonds. Soccer becomes more than just a game; it becomes a way to connect, support, and grow together as a family.

Positive Reinforcement and family involvement go a long way in early development

8.2 At-Home Soccer Activities for Families

One of the best ways to bring soccer into the home is through interactive drills. These can be done in your backyard, living room, or even a nearby park. Start with the "Pass and Move" drill, where family members pass the ball to each other and then quickly move to a new position. This drill not only improves passing accuracy but also encourages constant movement and spatial awareness. Next, set up a "Target Practice" using household items like laundry baskets or cardboard boxes as goalposts. Challenge each other to see who can score the most points by hitting the targets. Finally, the "Keepy-Uppy" challenge is a fantastic way to work on ball control. The goal is to keep the ball in the air using any part of the body except the hands. It's a fun, competitive game that can be played indoors with a soft ball or outside with a regular soccer ball. I would often allow my son, at a young age to dribble his mini ball inside the house (much to his mother's dismay). The object of the game was to NOT let the ball touch any furniture for 24 hours, and he would get a prize. This game continued until he was well into his middle school year; however, he was always one of the best dribblers on the field as a result!

Creating your own soccer equipment can also add a layer of creativity and fun to your at-home activities. You don't need professional gear to practice effectively. For instance, you can create goals using laundry baskets or cardboard boxes. These makeshift goals are easy to set up and move around, making them perfect for spontaneous games. Cones can be made from plastic bottles or cups, which can be used to set up dribbling courses or mark boundaries for small-sided games. If you're playing indoors, use socks or soft balls for dribbling practice to avoid breaking anything. These DIY solutions are not only cost-effective but also involve the whole family in the preparation process, adding another layer of engagement.

Family soccer games are another great way to bring everyone together. "Soccer Golf" is a fun game where you set up obstacles around the yard, and family members try to navigate a soccer ball through them, aiming for a target like a bucket or a small goal. This game combines elements of soccer and mini-golf, making it exciting for all ages. Another idea is a "Penalty Shootout" competition. Rotate the role of the goalkeeper among family members and see who can score the most goals. This game helps improve shooting accuracy and goalkeeping skills while keeping the competition friendly. For a more comprehensive challenge, set up a "Soccer Obstacle Course" with timed challenges. Use cones, ropes, and other household items to create a course that tests dribbling, passing, and shooting skills. Time each family member to see who can complete the course the fastest.

Soccer Golf and Family Obstacle Course

Keepy Uppy Game

Skill development challenges can motivate family members to practice and improve together. Start with daily dribbling challenges, where each family member practices dribbling for a set amount of time each day. Keep a progress chart to track improvements and celebrate milestones. Passing accuracy contests can also be a fun way to practice. Set up targets and see who can hit them the most times in a row. This not only improves passing skills but also adds a competitive element to the practice. Juggling competitions are another great way to develop ball control. See who can keep the ball in the air the longest using their feet, knees, and heads. These challenges encourage regular practice and create a sense of achievement as each family member improves.

To add an interactive element, consider creating a family soccer journal. Each family member can document their progress, challenges, and achievements. This journal can include photos, drawings, and notes about each practice session. It's a great way to reflect on improvements and create lasting memories. You can also use the journal to set new goals and track progress over time. This activity not only encourages skill development but also fosters a sense of accountability and pride in each family member's achievements.

One evening, after a particularly energetic session of "Keepy-Uppy," we decided to create a simple progress chart. Each family member had their name and a column for recording the number of consecutive touches. Over the weeks, we watched as the numbers grew, and so did the excitement. It became a daily ritual, and even our youngest, who started with just two touches, managed to reach ten. The sense of accomplishment and the shared joy was incredible.

In another instance, we set up a "Soccer Obstacle Course" in the backyard. Using cones, ropes, and even a garden hose, we created a winding path that required dribbling, quick turns, and precise passes. Each family member took turns timing their runs, and the friendly competition brought out the best in everyone. The course became more challenging as we added new obstacles, but the sense of fun and achievement remained constant. These activities not only improved our soccer skills but also brought us closer together as a family.

For one of our "Penalty Shootout" competitions, we decided to add a twist. Each goal scored had to be celebrated with a unique dance move. It led to some hilarious and memorable moments, with everyone coming up with creative and often funny celebrations. The laughter and camaraderie made the practice session feel less like training and more like a fun family game. It was a reminder that soccer, at its core, is about enjoyment and connection.

Incorporating these at-home soccer activities into your routine can significantly enhance your family's engagement with the sport. Whether it's through interactive drills, DIY equipment, fun games, or skill challenges, each activity offers a unique way to practice and bond. Soccer becomes more than just a game; it becomes a shared passion that brings the family together.

8.3 Discussing Soccer Values and Lessons at Home

One evening, after a particularly intense game, we gathered around the dinner table to talk about what had happened on the field. The conversation naturally flowed into a discussion about teamwork and cooperation. I shared stories of famous teams that achieved incredible success through their collective effort. Take the 1999 U.S. Women's National Team, for instance. Their World Cup victory wasn't just about individual talent; it was about how they worked together, supported each other, and executed their strategy as a unit. Encouraging your child to share their own experiences of teamwork during games can be enlightening. Ask them how they helped a teammate or how they felt when a teammate supported them. These discussions can reinforce the importance of working together, not just in soccer but in all aspects of life. Family discussions about the importance of cooperation can create a deeper understanding of how everyone's effort contributes to the overall success, fostering a sense of unity and shared purpose.

Promoting good sportsmanship is another crucial value to discuss at home. Role-playing scenarios can be an effective way to teach and reinforce these lessons. For example, act out a situation where someone loses a game but still congratulates the winner, and then contrast it with someone who reacts poorly. Discuss the differences and why good sportsmanship matters. Rewarding sportsmanship in family games can also be impactful. If someone shows kindness, fairness, or respect during a game, acknowledge it with praise or a small reward. This positive reinforcement encourages similar behavior in the future. It's also important to discuss the importance of respecting opponents, referees, and teammates. Explain that everyone is there to enjoy the game and improve, and treating others with respect is key to creating a positive environment. These conversations can help your child understand that sportsmanship isn't just about how you play the game,but also about how you treat others.

Handling wins and losses gracefully is a lesson that extends far beyond the soccer field. When discussing victories, focus on the effort and improvement rather than just the outcome. Celebrate the hard work that led to the win and the skills that were developed along the way. This approach helps children understand that success is a result of their dedication and effort. Conversely, use losses as opportunities to learn and grow. Ask your child what they think went wrong and what they could do differently next time.

Encourage them to express their feelings about the game, whether it's frustration, disappointment, or determination to improve. These discussions can help them process their emotions and develop a growth mindset, understanding that setbacks are a natural part of learning and improvement. It's crucial to create an environment where they feel safe to express their feelings and know that it's okay to make mistakes.

Setting personal and team goals can be a powerful way to foster a growth mindset in young athletes. Help your child set achievable soccer-related goals, whether it's improving their dribbling skills, increasing their stamina, or learning a new move. Discuss the importance of working towards these goals and the sense of accomplishment that comes from achieving them. It's also beneficial to set team goals. Talk about what the team wants to achieve and how each member can contribute to that success. Regularly review and adjust these goals based on progress. Celebrate milestones and reassess if goals need to be modified. This practice teaches children to be flexible and persistent, understanding that growth is a continuous process. It also emphasizes the importance of working together towards a common objective, reinforcing the values of teamwork and cooperation.

I remember when we first started setting goals with my own kids. We sat down with a notebook and wrote out both personal and team goals. Each week, we would review them and discuss what went well and what needed more work. The process was incredibly rewarding. Not only did it help them improve their skills, but it also gave them a sense of direction and purpose. It taught them that achieving a goal requires planning, effort, and sometimes adjusting the plan along the way. **My oldest still uses this technique today, and he is in college!**

One weekend, we decided to role-play different sportsmanship scenarios. We acted out a situation where one of us lost a game but still congratulated the winner with a smile. Then, we switched roles and acted out a poor reaction to losing. The kids found it amusing but also insightful. We discussed why showing good sportsmanship is important and how it affects everyone involved. It was a fun and educational activity that left a lasting impression on them.

Another time, after a tough loss, we gathered in the living room to talk about the game. I encouraged the kids to express their feelings and share what they thought went wrong. They were initially hesitant, but as we talked, they opened up.

We discussed what they could learn from the experience and how they could improve in the future. It was a valuable conversation that helped them see losses as part of the learning process.

Setting goals became a regular practice in our household. We created a goal chart and placed it on the fridge. Each child had their own set of goals, along with team goals for their soccer team. Every week, we would review the chart, celebrate achievements, and set new goals if needed. This practice instilled a sense of accountability and motivation in them, reinforcing the importance of continuous improvement.

These discussions and activities at home can significantly impact your child's understanding of soccer values and lessons. By emphasizing teamwork, promoting sportsmanship, handling wins and losses gracefully, and setting personal and team goals, you can help them develop not only as soccer players but also as individuals who value effort, respect, and growth.

8.4 SUPPORTING YOUR CHILD WITHOUT OVERSTEPPING

Balancing support and independence is a delicate act. I recall a time when my child, eager to improve, wanted to practice penalty kicks relentlessly. My instinct was to guide him through each step, but I realized he needed space to explore and learn on his own. Encouraging self-reflection and decision-making is crucial. Instead of dictating actions, ask open-ended questions like, "What do you think went well?" or "How could you improve that kick?" This approach helps children develop critical thinking and self-assessment skills. Providing guidance without taking control allows them to take ownership of their soccer experience. Encourage them to set their own goals and celebrate their milestones, fostering a sense of autonomy and confidence.

Effective communication with coaches plays a pivotal role in supporting your child's development. Attending parent-coach meetings is a great opportunity to build a rapport with the coach. Ask constructive questions about your child's progress and the team's overall strategy. Showing respect for the coach's decisions and strategies is essential. Coaches have a holistic view of the team and make decisions based on what they believe is best for everyone. If you have feedback or updates about your child's progress at home, share them with the coach in a respectful manner. This collaborative approach ensures that both you and the coach are on the same page, working together to support your child's development.

Recognizing burnout and stress in young athletes is vital for their well-being. I remember a season when my child, once enthusiastic about every practice, started dragging his feet and seemed disinterested. Noticing changes in enthusiasm or performance is the first step. If your child shows signs of fatigue, irritability, or a decline in performance, it might indicate burnout. Encourage rest and recovery time, emphasizing that it's okay to take breaks. Rest is as important as practice for young athletes. If the signs persist, seeking professional advice from a coach, sports psychologist, or pediatrician can provide additional support and guidance. Addressing these issues early helps prevent long-term negative effects and ensures that soccer remains a positive experience for your child.

Creating a positive home environment is foundational for nurturing young athletes. Encouraging healthy eating and sleeping habits is a good starting point. Balanced nutrition and adequate rest are crucial for physical and mental performance. Providing emotional support and understanding goes a long way. Be there to listen, offer encouragement, and validate their feelings, whether they're celebrating a win or coping with a loss. Celebrating non-soccer-related achievements and activities is also important. Acknowledge and celebrate their efforts in school, hobbies, and other interests. This holistic approach helps them feel valued and balanced, reinforcing that their worth extends beyond the soccer field.

One evening after a particularly tough game, my child was visibly upset. Instead of offering solutions, I simply sat with him and listened. He expressed his frustrations, and I validated his feelings. We then talked about what he could learn from the experience. This moment of emotional support and understanding strengthened our bond and helped him see setbacks as opportunities for growth. Encouraging self-reflection and decision-making in these moments fosters resilience and independence.

Effective communication with coaches can also make a significant difference. During a parent-coach meeting, I asked the coach about specific areas my child could work on at home. The coach appreciated the interest and provided valuable insights. Respecting the coach's decisions and strategies, even when they differ from your perspective, shows your child the importance of teamwork and trust in leadership. This collaborative approach helps create a unified support system for your child. Always remember that the coach is in charge of the team, and it takes good communication during the early stages of development to make sure the family's and coach's goals are similar for the player.

Creating a positive home environment extends beyond soccer. We made it a point to celebrate all achievements, whether it was a good grade in school or learning a new skill.

This holistic approach helped my child feel valued in all areas of life, reinforcing that their worth isn't tied solely to soccer performance. Encouraging healthy eating and sleeping habits also played a significant role. We established routines that included balanced meals and regular bedtimes, ensuring they were well-rested and nourished for both school and soccer.

By balancing support with independence, communicating effectively with coaches, recognizing burnout and stress, and creating a positive home environment, you can provide a nurturing and supportive foundation for your young athlete. These strategies ensure that your child feels valued, supported, and empowered to grow both on and off the soccer field.

In the next chapter, we'll explore advanced tips and techniques to elevate your child's soccer skills, focusing on specific drills and strategies for different positions.

9. Overcoming Common Challenges

One rainy afternoon, we were midway through practice when I noticed the kids starting to lose focus. The drills seemed monotonous to them, and their energy was waning. I paused the session and decided to try something different. I told the kids to imagine they were pirates searching for hidden treasure on a deserted island. The soccer ball became the treasure, and the field transformed into an exciting landscape filled with obstacles. Suddenly, their eyes lit up, and the energy surged back into the field. That day, I learned the importance of keeping young players engaged through creativity and play.

9.1 Keeping Young Players Engaged

Understanding the short attention spans of young players is crucial for designing effective training sessions. Kids, especially those under ten, have limited attention spans and can quickly become disinterested if activities drag on too long. To keep them focused, structure your activities in small, varied segments. Instead of spending thirty minutes on a single drill, break it down into shorter, five to ten-minute segments. This not only keeps their attention but also allows them to experience a variety of skills and movements within one session. Use colorful, engaging equipment like brightly colored cones, fun markers, and small goals. These visual stimuli capture their interest and make the activities feel more like play than training. Rotating activities frequently is another key strategy. If you notice the kids losing interest, switch to a different drill or game. This keeps the practice dynamic and prevents boredom.

Incorporating play and creativity into training sessions can make a significant difference in keeping young players engaged. Themed games, like the pirate adventure I mentioned earlier, are incredibly effective. You can create various themes such as superheroes, space explorers, or zoo animals to keep the kids excited and engaged. Allowing players to invent their own drills is another great way to foster creativity. Give them the freedom to set up their own obstacle courses or come up with new games. This not only keeps them engaged but also empowers them to take ownership of their learning. Including free play periods in your sessions can also be beneficial. Let the kids have some time to play without structured drills or instructions. This unstructured time allows them to explore their creativity and develop a genuine love for the game.

Positive reinforcement plays a critical role in keeping young players motivated and engaged. Offering praise and encouragement, even for small achievements, boosts their confidence and keeps them eager to learn. Simple phrases like "Great job!" or "I love how you dribbled the ball!" can have a profound impact on their self-esteem. Using rewards and recognition can also motivate them. Create a reward system where kids earn stickers or small prizes for their efforts and improvements. Recognize their achievements publicly during practice or games to make them feel valued. Providing constructive feedback is equally important. Instead of focusing solely on what they did wrong, highlight what they did well and offer specific suggestions for improvement. This balanced approach helps them learn and grow without feeling discouraged.

Interactive and cooperative activities foster engagement through teamwork and collaboration. Partner drills with shared goals encourage players to work together and support each other. For example, pair up players to complete a passing drill, where they must make a certain number of successful passes to achieve a goal. This not only improves their passing skills but also teaches them the importance of teamwork. Team challenges that require collaboration, such as relay races or small-sided games, can be very effective. These activities create a sense of camaraderie and make the training sessions more enjoyable. Interactive storytelling games related to soccer can also be a hit. Create a story where the players are characters who must complete various soccer-related tasks to progress. This adds an element of adventure and keeps them engaged while practicing their skills.

One memorable practice session involved a game where the kids had to navigate an obstacle course while pretending to be secret agents on a mission. They had to dribble the ball through cones, pass it accurately to a teammate, and then shoot at a target to complete their mission. The excitement and laughter were contagious, and the kids were fully engaged throughout the session. This experience reinforced the importance of incorporating creativity, play, and positive reinforcement into our training sessions. By understanding their attention spans, structuring activities in varied segments, and fostering a supportive and interactive environment, we can keep young players engaged and motivated to learn and grow in the game of soccer.

Interactive Element: Designing Your Own Drill

Give players the opportunity to design their own drill. Provide them with some basic equipment like cones, balls, and markers, and let them come up with a new game or drill. Encourage them to explain the rules and demonstrate it to the group. This not only keeps them engaged but also fosters creativity and leadership skills.

9.2 Balancing Fun and Learning

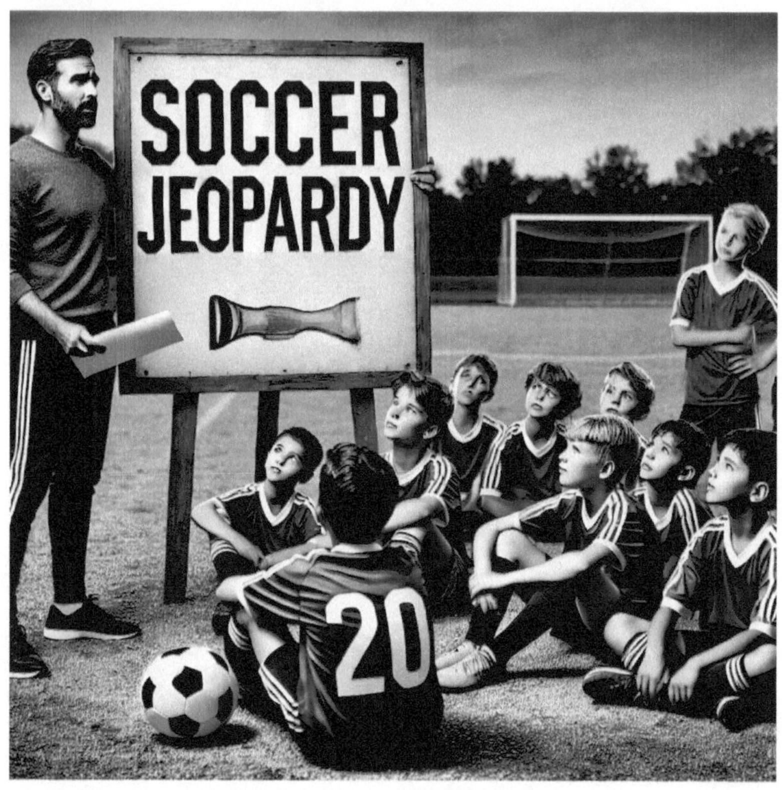

One brisk autumn afternoon, as the leaves began to fall, I decided to mix things up during our practice session. I gathered the kids around and explained that today, we would be learning soccer rules through a game called "Soccer Jeopardy." Each correct answer would earn their team points, and the team with the most points would get an extra ten minutes of free play at the end of practice. The excitement was palpable, and the kids were eager to participate. This approach seamlessly integrated educational elements into our training, making learning a natural part of their play.

Using games to teach soccer rules implicitly is a fantastic way to keep young players engaged while ensuring they understand the basics. For instance, a game like "Penalty Shootout Trivia" can combine the excitement of shooting goals with answering questions about the rules of the game. This method reinforces their knowledge without making it feel like a classroom lesson. Another effective strategy is incorporating math or literacy into soccer drills. You can set up a simple passing drill where each successful pass earns a point, and the kids have to keep track of their scores. This not only improves their math skills but also adds an element of competition and fun. Storytelling that includes soccer lessons can also be incredibly engaging. Create a narrative where the players are characters in a story, and they must complete various soccer-related tasks to advance the plot. This approach makes learning feel like an adventure, keeping the kids captivated and motivated.

Creating enjoyable learning experiences is crucial for fostering a positive attitude towards soccer. Designing drills that feel like games is an excellent way to achieve this. For example, you can turn a simple dribbling drill into a game of "Dribble Tag," where one player is "it" and has to tag others by dribbling close to them. This not only makes the drill more fun but also encourages players to think creatively and develop their skills in a playful environment. Encouraging laughter and fun during practice is equally important. Don't be afraid to be silly or make jokes. When kids see that their coach is having fun, they're more likely to relax and enjoy themselves. This positive atmosphere makes them more receptive to learning and trying new things.

Adapting activities to meet the individual needs and interests of each player is essential for keeping them engaged and motivated. Offering multiple skill levels within the same drill can help accommodate different abilities. For example, in a passing drill, you can set up different distances for players to pass the ball. Beginners can start with shorter distances, while more advanced players can challenge themselves with longer passes. This ensures that everyone is working at their own level and feels a sense of accomplishment. Allowing players to choose some activities can also be empowering. Give them options and let them decide what they want to work on. This sense of autonomy makes them feel more invested in their training and more motivated to improve.

Balancing structured drills with unstructured playtime is vital for maintaining a positive and engaging training environment. Scheduled free play sessions give kids the opportunity to explore their creativity and practice their skills in a relaxed setting. For example, set aside the last ten minutes of practice for free play, where the kids can choose what they want to do. This unstructured time allows them to experiment and discover new ways to enjoy the game. Opportunities for spontaneous games can also be beneficial. If you notice that the kids are getting restless or losing focus, take a break from structured drills and organize a quick, fun game. This spontaneous play can re-energize them and make the rest of the practice session more productive.

One memorable session involved a game called "Math Soccer," where each successful pass required the kids to solve a simple math problem. The players were divided into teams, and each correct answer earned their team a point. The kids were so engrossed in the game that they didn't even realize they were practicing their math skills. Another time, we used storytelling to teach defensive positioning. I told the kids a story about a knight protecting a castle, and they had to use their defensive skills to keep the "invaders" (other players) from reaching the goal. These experiences demonstrated that integrating educational elements into fun activities can make learning enjoyable and effective.

Balancing fun and learning in soccer is about creating an environment where kids are excited to participate and motivated to improve. By integrating educational elements into fun activities, creating enjoyable learning experiences, adapting to individual needs, and balancing structured and unstructured time, we can foster a love for the game and help young players develop their skills while having fun.

9.3 Simplifying Complex Soccer Concepts

One evening, I watched a group of kids struggle to understand the offside rule. Their eyes glazed over as I explained, and I realized I needed a different approach. Breaking down complex soccer concepts into simple, manageable parts is crucial for young players. Start with step-by-step instructions. Instead of explaining the entire offside rule at once, break it down. First, explain what "offside" means. Then, show them where they need to be on the field to stay onside.

Use simple language and avoid jargon. Kids might not understand terms like "defensive line" or "last man." Instead, say, "You can't be closer to the goal than the second-to-last defender when the ball is passed to you." Demonstrate concepts visually. Use cones, markers, or even other players to show what "offside" looks like. A visual representation helps kids grasp the concept better than words alone.

Using analogies and comparisons can make complex ideas more relatable and understandable. Compare soccer strategies to familiar activities. For example, explain positioning using the analogy of chess. Just like in chess, each player has a specific role and must be in the right place to support the team. Use everyday examples to explain positioning. Compare a midfielder's role to that of a traffic cop, directing the flow of traffic (the ball) and ensuring everything moves smoothly. Relate soccer movements to animal behaviors. For instance, describe a defender moving to cover an attacker as a tiger stalking its prey. These analogies make abstract concepts more concrete and easier for kids to understand.

Using analogies also proved effective during another session. I explained the role of a midfielder by comparing it to a chef in a busy kitchen. Just like a chef manages orders, ingredients, and the timing of dishes, a midfielder manages the ball, teammates, and the flow of the game. The kids found this comparison relatable and could visualize the midfielder's responsibilities more clearly.

Interactive learning tools can also simplify complex soccer concepts. Interactive whiteboards are fantastic for visual demonstrations. You can draw plays, show movement patterns, and highlight key areas on the field. Soccer-specific apps with animated drills are another great resource. These apps break down skills into easy-to-follow steps and provide visual and auditory instructions. Kids can watch the animations, follow along, and practice the drills at their own pace. These tools make learning interactive and engaging, helping kids grasp complex concepts more effectively.

Reinforcing complex concepts through repetition and varied practice is essential. Repeat drills with incremental complexity. Start with a basic drill, and once the kids are comfortable, add a new layer of complexity. For example, begin with a simple passing drill, and then introduce a defender to add pressure. Review concepts in different contexts. If you're teaching defensive positioning, practice it in various scenarios—during a scrimmage, in a one-on-one drill, or in a small-sided game. This varied practice helps kids apply the concept in different situations. Use consistent terminology. If you call a certain move "the cutback," always refer to it as "the cutback." Consistency helps reinforce learning and makes it easier for kids to remember and apply what they've learned. Rinse and repeat as much as possible!

One practice session, I used an interactive whiteboard to explain the concept of "zonal marking." I drew a soccer field and used different colors to show each player's zone. The kids watched as I moved the markers around, demonstrating how they should shift and cover their zones. Then, we practiced it on the field, starting with a basic drill and gradually increasing the complexity. By the end of the session, they had a much better understanding of zonal marking. This experience taught me the value of using interactive tools and breaking down complex concepts into manageable steps.

Repetition and varied practice also played a significant role in another session focused on shooting under pressure. We started with simple one-on-one drills, where the kids had to shoot while being defended. As they became more comfortable, we introduced small-sided games with added defenders. This incremental complexity helped them apply the concept in different contexts and improved their ability to perform under pressure. **Starting out by explaining the concept of the day, create drills to incorporate that concept, then progress to game-style situations and practice the concept in full speed. This is how top-level coaches prepare their training sessions, and this is the best way to reinforce ideas for the entire session!**

Simplifying complex soccer concepts involves breaking them down into simple, manageable parts, using analogies and comparisons, incorporating interactive learning tools, and reinforcing through repetition and varied practice. These strategies make abstract concepts more concrete and easier for young players to understand and apply on the field. By taking this approach, we can help kids develop a deeper understanding of the game and improve their skills in a fun and engaging way.

Interactive Element: Analogies Activity

Have players come up with their own analogies for different soccer concepts. For example, ask them to compare defending to something they do in their everyday lives. This activity helps them relate complex ideas to familiar experiences, reinforcing their understanding.

9.4 HANDLING PARENTAL EXPECTATIONS AND PRESSURE

One crisp autumn evening, I held a meeting with the parents of our team. The air was filled with excitement and a bit of tension. Many parents had high hopes for their young athletes, dreaming of scholarships and professional careers. While these dreams are valid, managing parental expectations is essential to ensure that the focus remains on the child's enjoyment and development. Setting clear, achievable goals for players helps align parental expectations with a realistic view of youth soccer. For instance, rather than aiming for a college scholarship or pro contract at age six, set goals like improving dribbling skills or enjoying the game. Communicate the importance of enjoying the game over winning by emphasizing the value of effort and improvement. Encourage parents to celebrate their child's progress, no matter how small, and to focus on the joy of playing rather than just the outcomes. This shift in mindset helps reduce pressure and fosters a more supportive environment for young athletes.

Effective communication with parents is key to managing expectations and ensuring everyone is on the same page. Regular updates and feedback sessions allow parents to stay informed about their child's progress and areas for improvement. These sessions also provide an opportunity for parents to ask questions and voice concerns. Open lines of communication are essential for building trust and transparency. Encourage parents to reach out with any questions or concerns they may have and be responsive to their inquiries. Group meetings are another effective way to discuss team goals and values. These meetings create a sense of community and allow everyone to align their expectations and support the team's objectives.

Educating parents on the stages of player development and realistic progress timelines is crucial for managing expectations. Share resources on youth soccer development, such as articles, books, or videos that explain the typical progression of skills and abilities at different ages. Provide examples of professional players' early development to illustrate that even the best athletes started with basic skills and gradually improved over time. Discuss the long-term benefits of focusing on fundamentals, such as enhanced technical abilities, better game understanding, and increased enjoyment of the sport. When parents understand that early specialization and pressure can hinder rather than help their child's development, they are more likely to adopt a supportive and realistic approach.

Creating a supportive environment that reduces pressure on young players is essential for their overall well-being and development. Encourage positive sidelines behavior by reminding parents that their role is to cheer and support, not to coach or criticize. Positive reinforcement from the sidelines can significantly boost a child's confidence and enjoyment of the game. Promote a team culture of support and encouragement by fostering a sense of camaraderie and unity among players and parents. Organize team-building activities and events that bring everyone together and strengthen the bonds within the team. Parent workshops on positive reinforcement can also be beneficial. These workshops provide parents with strategies for encouraging their children in a constructive and supportive manner. Topics can include effective praise, handling mistakes, and fostering a growth mindset.

One of the most memorable moments from my coaching career was when we organized a parent workshop focused on positive reinforcement. We discussed the importance of praising effort and improvement rather than just outcomes. Parents shared their experiences and concerns, and we brainstormed strategies for supporting their children in a positive way. The workshop ended with a sense of camaraderie and a commitment to creating a supportive environment for our young athletes. This experience reinforced the importance of educating and involving parents in the process of their child's development.

Another effective strategy is to involve parents in the training process. Invite them to participate in certain drills or activities during practice. This not only helps them understand what their children are learning but also gives them a firsthand experience of the challenges and joys of soccer. It fosters empathy and a deeper connection between parents and their children. Additionally, organizing family soccer days where parents, siblings, and children can play together can strengthen the family bond and create a more supportive environment for the young athletes.

Managing parental expectations and pressure involves setting clear, achievable goals, maintaining effective communication, educating parents on player development, and creating a supportive environment. By focusing on these strategies, we can ensure that young athletes enjoy the game, develop their skills, and thrive in a positive and encouraging environment.

As we move forward, it's essential to remember that soccer is not just about winning or achieving professional success; it's about fostering a love for the game, building character, and creating lasting memories. Setting realistic expectations with parent's like explaining that less than 1% of kids in the US will obtain scholarships to play in college and that number is way less for those that actually go pro, can sometimes open their eyes to a more realistic vision for their children. Next, we will explore how to prepare young athletes for competitive matches, ensuring they are ready both physically and mentally to perform at their best.

1% OF 1%
COLLEGE AND PRO
CONTRACTS

10. Advanced Tips and Techniques

One sweltering afternoon, I found myself in the middle of an intense training session, surrounded by eager young players. Despite the heat, their enthusiasm was palpable. Among them was a boy named Ethan, whose dribbling skills were already impressive for his age. But Ethan wanted to take his game to the next level. He asked me, "Coach, how can I dribble like the pros?" That question set the stage for a series of advanced dribbling drills that transformed not just Ethan's game, but the entire team's approach to ball control.

10.1 Advanced Dribbling and Ball Control

To elevate your dribbling skills, you need to embrace high-intensity drills that challenge your speed, control, and agility. One effective drill is the "Zigzag Sprint Drill." Set up a series of cones in a zigzag pattern and sprint through them while dribbling the ball. This drill forces you to make sharp turns and maintain control at high speeds. Another excellent exercise is the "Figure-Eight Dribbling" drill. Arrange two cones about five yards apart and dribble the ball around them in a figure-eight pattern. This drill enhances your ability to make tight turns and improves your overall ball control. For an added challenge, try the "Blindfolded Dribble." With a blindfold on, dribble the ball using only your sense of touch. This drill significantly enhances your tactile sensitivity and forces you to rely on your feet rather than your eyes.

Maintaining ball control under pressure is crucial in real-game situations. One effective technique is "Close Quarters Dribbling." Set up a small, confined space with cones and have a defender apply pressure as you dribble within the area. This drill improves your ability to maneuver in tight spaces while keeping the ball. Equally important is learning to shield the ball and turn against opponents. Practice "Shielding and Turning" by having a defender press against you while you protect the ball and look for an opportunity to turn and escape. This drill not only enhances your ball control but also builds physical resilience and strategic thinking.

Mastering combination moves can give you a significant edge over your opponents. One of my favorites is the "Step Over to Nutmeg" sequence. Begin with a stepover, then quickly follow it with a nutmeg (kicking the ball through the defender's legs). This move combines deception with precision, leaving defenders off-balance. Another powerful combination is the "Feint to Drag Back." Start with a body feint to mislead the defender, then use a dragback to change direction and accelerate past them. Practicing these moves regularly will increase your dribbling repertoire and make you more unpredictable on the field.

Encouraging creativity and flair in your dribbling can elevate your game to new heights. Dedicate time to "Freestyle Dribbling Sessions," where you experiment with different moves, tricks, and combinations. This freeform practice allows you to discover what works best for you and builds confidence in your abilities. Additionally, challenge yourself with the "Invent Your Own Move" exercise. Spend time creating a unique dribbling move, practice it until it becomes second nature, and then test it out in real-game situations. This not only makes you a more versatile player but also adds an element of surprise that can catch opponents off guard. To bring these concepts to life, let's incorporate an interactive element:

Interactive Element: Dribbling Challenge

Set up a series of cones in various patterns (zigzag, figure-eight, and confined spaces). Divide players into small groups and have them rotate through each station, practicing the drills discussed. At each station, encourage them to incorporate a combination move or invent a new one. Keep track of their progress and offer feedback on their technique and creativity.

By integrating these advanced dribbling drills and techniques into your training routine, you can significantly enhance your ball control, agility, and creativity on the field. Whether you're a young player like Ethan, a dedicated coach, or a supportive parent, these methods will give you the tools to elevate your game and enjoy the beautiful game of soccer even more.

10.2 Tactical Awareness and Game Intelligence

In every game, the ability to read the play is a skill that separates good players from great ones. Developing this ability involves pattern recognition drills. Imagine you're on the field, and the ball is constantly moving. You need to anticipate where it will go next. Start with drills that have you observe and predict the movement patterns of your teammates and opponents. For instance, set up a scrimmage where you focus solely on identifying and reacting to these patterns. Practicing game scenarios is another valuable tool. Simulate different game situations where you must make quick decisions based on the evolving play. Analyzing an opponent's play can also be insightful. Watch game footage, noting how opponents move and react in various situations. This helps you understand their strategies and anticipate their next moves.

Understanding formations is another crucial aspect of tactical awareness. Each formation has its own set of advantages and disadvantages. The 4-4-2 formation, for example, is well-balanced, providing a solid defense and a versatile attack. However, it can sometimes leave the midfield exposed. The 3-5-2 formation, with its emphasis on midfield dominance, allows for greater control of the game but requires highly disciplined wingbacks. On the other hand, the 4-3-3 formation is excellent for an attacking play, offering width and depth in the offensive phase, but it can leave the defense vulnerable to counter-attacks. Understanding these formations and their implications helps you adapt to various game scenarios and make more informed decisions on the field.

Decision-making skills are essential in soccer, and they can be honed through specific drills. One effective drill is "Pressure Passing with Options," where you practice making quick passes under pressure while having multiple passing options available. This drill forces you to think quickly and make the best decision in real-time. Small-sided games with a tactical focus are also beneficial. These games reduce the number of players, creating more opportunities for each player to make decisions and execute them. For example, a 3v3 or 4v4 game encourages quick passes, movement, and strategic thinking, all of which are crucial for improving decision-making skills.

I would often enter multiple teams into local 3v3 tournaments, which would serve as 'qualifiers" for national events. My higher-level players got the most value out of these long and challenging days because there is absolutely no where to hide in a very competitive 3v3 game. I found that entering teams in these tournaments from u7-u12 was extremely beneficial for higher-level players to handle competitive atmospheres, dealing with extreme pressure, and really honing in on dribbling and passing skills. My top teams would play up an age group and literally not score a point against older opposition for the first few years. Once they reached U10, they were unstoppable. They won almost every tournament they entered, including a few national competitions across the country. The players enjoyed the intense competition and gathering a large collection of medals and trophies. I, as a coach, enjoyed watching them develop into little soccer stars and carry those skills into the larger game of 11v11. I will also add that every one of those players is now either playing in college or pro somewhere. Not because of playing 3v3, but because we laid the right foundation for them as young players to accelerate their playing styles and IQ's at a very young age.

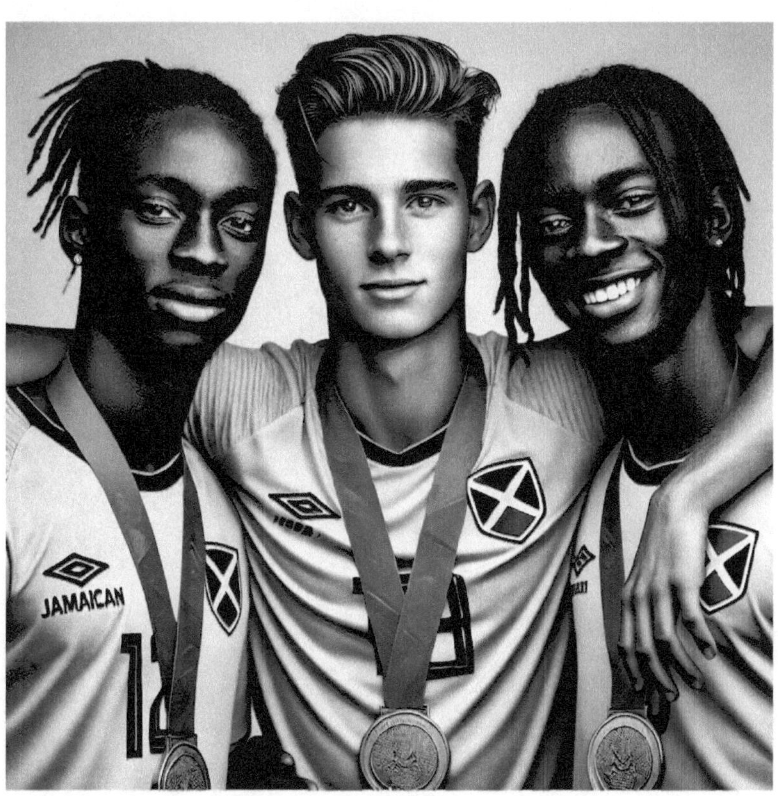

Positional play is about maintaining discipline and understanding spatial dynamics on the field. Zonal marking drills are essential for this. In these drills, you focus on defending your zone rather than marking a specific player. This helps you understand how to maintain your position and protect your area effectively. Positional rotation exercises are equally important. These exercises involve players rotating through different positions on the field, helping them understand the responsibilities and spatial dynamics of each role. This not only improves individual understanding but also enhances team cohesion and adaptability.

Interactive Element: Positional Awareness Exercise

Set up a small-sided game where players rotate positions every few minutes. This helps them understand the spatial dynamics and responsibilities of each role. Encourage them to communicate and work together to maintain the team's shape and effectiveness. This exercise not only improves individual tactical awareness but also fosters teamwork and communication.

10.3 Improving Physical Fitness and Conditioning

One Saturday morning, I watched the kids run around the field, their energy boundless. But energy alone isn't enough. To truly excel in soccer, players need a structured strength and conditioning program tailored to their needs. Body-weight exercises are a great place to start. Simple yet effective, exercises like push-ups, squats, and lunges build foundational strength without the need for equipment. As players advance, incorporating resistance band and parachute workouts can add another layer of challenge. These bands are versatile and perfect for enhancing muscle strength and flexibility. Core stability drills, such as planks and leg raises, are also crucial. A strong core not only improves balance but also helps in executing powerful kicks and quick turns.

Endurance training is another vital component. Soccer is a game of continuous movement, requiring players to maintain high energy levels throughout. Interval running is an excellent way to build this stamina. Alternate between short bursts of intense running and periods of rest. This mimics the stop-and-go nature of a soccer game. Fartlek training, which mixes continuous running with speed variations, also works wonders. It's less structured than interval training, making it more enjoyable for young players while still building their endurance.

Speed and agility are skills every soccer player needs. Ladder drills are a staple. Set up a ladder on the ground and have players run through it, focusing on quick, precise foot movements. Plyometric exercises, like box jumps and bounding, can also boost explosive power. These exercises train muscles to generate force quickly, crucial for sprints and sudden changes in direction. Sprint drills with changes of direction further enhance this agility. Set up cones in different patterns and have players sprint from one to another, changing direction rapidly. This not only improves speed but also teaches them to maintain control while moving quickly.

Flexibility and mobility exercises are essential for preventing injuries. Dynamic stretching routines should be a part of every warm-up. Unlike static stretches, dynamic stretches involve moving parts of your body, gradually increasing reach and speed. This prepares muscles for the demands of the game. Foam rolling techniques can also aid in recovery and injury prevention. Rolling out muscles helps reduce tightness and improve blood flow, keeping muscles pliable and ready for action.

These training techniques, from bodyweight exercises to dynamic stretching, form a comprehensive fitness regimen. They ensure young players are not just strong and fast but also resilient and flexible.

10.3 Using Data and Analytics in Youth Soccer

One afternoon, as I watched a group of young players practice, I realized how much potential lies in the integration of data and analytics into their training routines. Imagine being able to pinpoint exactly where a player needs improvement or how to tweak team strategies to exploit opponents' weaknesses. The advantages are immense. Data and analytics can significantly improve individual performance by providing detailed insights into a player's strengths and weaknesses. For instance, if you notice a player consistently faltering in speed during the latter part of a game, you can tailor their training to build endurance. Moreover, analytics enhance team strategies by identifying patterns in both your team and the opposition's play, allowing for more effective game plans. This level of insight helps in identifying specific areas where players excel and where they need further development.

To track player performance, several methods stand out. GPS tracking devices are invaluable. These devices monitor a player's movements, distance covered, and speed during a game. With this data, you can assess whether a player is maintaining their positioning or if they need to improve their stamina. Heart rate monitors add another layer of insight, helping you understand how a player's body responds to the physical demands of the game. This information is crucial for tailoring conditioning programs. Performance analysis software takes it a step further by compiling all this data into easily digestible reports. These tools offer a comprehensive view of a player's performance, highlighting areas for improvement and tracking progress over time.

Analyzing game data to improve team performance is another critical aspect. Video analysis software is a game-changer. By recording matches and practices, you can review footage to identify tactical errors, positioning issues, and missed opportunities. This visual feedback is invaluable for both players and coaches. Statistical analysis tools complement video analysis by providing quantitative data. For example, you can track the number of successful passes, shots on goal, and defensive blocks. This data helps in making informed decisions about training focus and game strategies.

Implementing technology in your training sessions can seem daunting, but it doesn't have to be. Start by using apps for skill tracking. These apps can log individual player stats, track progress, and set specific training goals. Interactive training programs are another excellent resource. These programs offer drills and exercises tailored to individual needs, complete with video tutorials and progress tracking. By incorporating these technologies, you create a more engaging and effective training environment.

Interactive Element: Performance Analysis Exercise

After a match, gather the team to review key moments using video analysis software. Focus on specific plays, discuss what went well, and identify areas for improvement. Encourage players to share their observations and learn from each other's insights. This exercise not only enhances understanding but also fosters a collaborative learning atmosphere.

Integrating data and analytics into youth soccer training brings a new level of precision and effectiveness. It allows you to tailor training programs to individual needs, improve team strategies, and track progress with unprecedented accuracy. By embracing these technologies, you equip young players with the tools they need to excel on the field.

10.4 PREPARING FOR COMPETITIVE MATCHES

One of the most exciting yet nerve-wracking aspects of coaching youth soccer is preparing for competitive matches. The anticipation is palpable, and the key to success often lies in meticulous pre-match preparation. A well-structured warm-up routine can set the tone. Start with light jogging to get the blood flowing, followed by dynamic stretches targeting key muscle groups. Incorporate ball work to get the players' feet moving and minds focused. Another critical component is mental preparation. Encourage players to visualize their roles and responsibilities on the field. This mental rehearsal can boost confidence and reduce anxiety. Tactical briefings are equally important. Gather the team and outline the game plan. Discuss the formation, key strategies, and roles. Ensure each player understands their task, whether it's marking a specific opponent or making runs into space.

In-game strategies require adaptability and quick thinking. Being able to adjust formations mid-game can be a game-changer. If the opposition is exploiting your flanks, consider shifting to a formation that provides more width and defensive cover. Communicate these adjustments clearly and ensure players understand their new roles. Utilizing substitutions strategically is another vital element. Keep an eye on fatigue levels and performance. Substitutions can be used to inject fresh energy into the game or to change tactics. For example, bringing on a fast winger can stretch the opposition's defense and create more scoring opportunities.

Post-match analysis is where the real learning happens. Start by reviewing game footage, focusing on key moments that influenced the game's outcome. This visual feedback helps players see what they did well and where they can improve. Performance feedback sessions are crucial. Gather the team and discuss individual and collective performances. Be constructive, highlighting positives while offering specific areas for improvement. Identify patterns, such as recurring defensive lapses or missed scoring opportunities, and tailor future training sessions to address these issues.

Recovery protocols are often overlooked but are essential for maintaining performance and preventing injuries. Begin with cool-down exercises immediately after the match. Light jogging and static stretching help reduce muscle stiffness and promote recovery. Hydration and nutrition are also vital. Encourage players to rehydrate with water or sports drinks and consume a balanced meal rich in protein and carbohydrates. Active recovery techniques, such as light swimming or yoga, can further aid in muscle recovery and relaxation. These methods help players bounce back quickly and be ready for the next training session or match. I introduced cryotherapy to my high-level athletes at a very young age and found extreme benefits for them. It's basically bringing the body temperature to low levels in short period of time. This enables the body to reduce swelling both internally and externally, helping with muscle fatigue, cramping, and overuse.

Incorporating these detailed strategies into your approach will not only prepare your team physically but also mentally and tactically for competitive matches. The holistic preparation encompassing warm-ups, mental readiness, tactical adjustments, post-match analysis, and recovery ensures your players are ready to face any challenge on the field.

10.5 Injury Prevention and Recovery Strategies

One humid summer day, I was coaching a spirited match when one of our best players, Jack, suddenly crumpled to the ground, clutching his ankle. Instantly, the atmosphere grew tense. Ankle sprains are among the most common soccer injuries, often occurring from sudden twists or awkward landings. They can be prevented through balance and stability drills, which strengthen the muscles around the ankle. Exercises like standing on one leg or using a balance board can make a significant difference. Another frequent injury is hamstring strains, often the result of overstretching or muscle fatigue. Strengthening weak areas with targeted exercises, such as hamstring curls and lunges, can help. Knee ligament injuries, particularly ACL tears, are also prevalent and can be devastating. Preventative measures include dynamic warm-up routines that incorporate exercises like high knees, butt kicks, and lateral shuffles to enhance flexibility and muscle coordination.

When injuries do occur, immediate response is critical. The RICE method—Rest, Ice, Compression, Elevation—is a go-to strategy for managing acute injuries. Rest the injured area to prevent further damage, apply ice to reduce swelling, use compression wraps to support the injury, and elevate the limb to minimize swelling. On-field assessment techniques are also vital. Quickly determine the severity of the injury by checking for deformities, swelling, and the range of motion. If the injury appears serious, such as a suspected fracture or severe ligament tear, it's essential to seek professional medical help immediately.

Rehabilitation programs are crucial for a safe return to play. Physiotherapy sessions provide structured recovery plans tailored to the specific injury. These sessions often include exercises to restore strength, flexibility, and range of motion. Gradual return to activity is another key aspect. Start with low-impact exercises and slowly reintroduce soccer-specific drills. Monitoring progress is essential to ensuring the player is recovering as expected. Keep track of pain levels, swelling, and functional performance. Adjust the rehabilitation plan as needed based on these observations.

Incorporating balance and stability drills into regular training can significantly reduce the risk of ankle sprains. Exercises like single-leg stands, where players balance on one foot for a set period, can strengthen the stabilizing muscles around the ankle. Using a balance board can add an extra challenge and improve proprioception. For hamstring strains, strengthening exercises are crucial. Hamstring curls, where players lie on their stomachs and lift their heels towards their buttocks, can build the necessary muscle strength. Lunges, both forward and reverse, also help in strengthening the hamstrings and improving overall leg stability.

Dynamic warm-up routines play a vital role in preventing knee ligament injuries. Incorporate exercises like high knees, which involve lifting the knees towards the chest while jogging in place, and butt kicks, where players kick their heels towards their buttocks. Lateral shuffles, which involve side-stepping quickly, can enhance flexibility and coordination. These exercises prepare the muscles and ligaments for the physical demands of soccer, reducing the risk of injuries.

Ensuring players follow the RICE method immediately after an injury can significantly impact their recovery time. Resting the injured area prevents further damage, while applying ice helps reduce swelling and pain. Compression wraps provide support and limit swelling, and elevating the limb minimizes swelling by reducing blood flow to the area. On-field assessment techniques involve quickly evaluating the injury to determine its severity. Check for visible deformities, swelling, and the player's ability to move the injured area. If the injury appears severe, such as a suspected fracture or a severe ligament tear, seeking professional medical help promptly is crucial.

Physiotherapy sessions are an integral part of effective rehabilitation programs. These sessions include exercises tailored to the specific injury, focusing on restoring strength, flexibility, and range of motion. Gradual return to activity involves starting with low-impact exercises and slowly reintroducing soccer-specific drills. Monitoring progress is essential to ensuring the player is recovering as expected. Keep track of pain levels, swelling, and functional performance. Adjust the rehabilitation plan as needed based on these observations.

10.6 Long-Term Player Development Pathways

When I first started coaching, I quickly realized that setting long-term development goals for players is pivotal. These goals aren't just about immediate success; they're about building a foundation for the future. Individual skill milestones are essential. For instance, a young player might aim to improve their dribbling accuracy or master a specific type of pass. Physical development targets are equally important. This could mean enhancing endurance, building muscle strength, or increasing flexibility. Tactical understanding objectives should not be overlooked either. Understanding game strategies and positioning can significantly impact a player's effectiveness on the field. By setting these varied goals, players can see a clear path forward, making their progression tangible and motivating.

Creating comprehensive development plans tailored to each player can make a huge difference. Personalized training schedules are the first step. These schedules should consider the player's current skill level, areas for improvement, and personal goals. Progress tracking systems are vital. Regularly updating these systems allows players and coaches to see how far they've come and where they need to focus next. This could be as simple as a journal where players note their daily or weekly progress or more sophisticated apps that track various metrics. Having a structured plan helps players stay focused and committed, knowing that every practice brings them closer to their long-term goals.

Balancing academics and soccer can be a real challenge, but it's crucial for young athletes. Time management techniques are essential here. Encourage players to create a weekly schedule that includes schoolwork, soccer practices, and relaxation time. Using tools like planners or digital calendars can help them manage their time effectively. Support systems for student-athletes are also important. This could involve working with teachers to ensure they understand the player's commitments or finding a mentor who has success-fully balanced both academics and sports. Maintaining a balance ensures that players can excel both on the field and in the classroom without feeling overwhelmed.

For those aspiring to reach professional levels, under-standing the pathways to professional soccer is key. Joining soccer academies can provide structured training and expo-sure to high-level coaching. These academies often have connections to professional clubs, offering a direct route to the pros. Scouting and recruitment processes are another crucial aspect. Players need to understand what scouts are looking for and how to showcase their skills effectively. Networking and exposure opportunities can also play a significant role. Participating in high-profile tournaments, attending soccer camps, and connecting with coaches and scouts can open doors to professional opportunities. Each of these steps requires dedication and strategic planning but can lead to exciting career prospects in soccer. **This is some-thing we will dive much deeper into with our next edition of "The Soccer Success Playbook" series.**

Incorporating these elements into a player's development plan ensures a holistic approach. It's not just about the physical skills, but also understanding the game, balancing life commitments, and seizing opportunities. As we wrap up this chapter, remember that the journey to soccer excellence is multifaceted, involving personal goals, structured plans, balanced life, and strategic pathways.

Conclusion

As we reach the conclusion of "The Soccer Success Playbook: Early Age Development Edition," I hope that this journey has been both enlightening and practical for you. My vision for this book was to provide a roadmap for parents, coaches, and young players navigating the intricate landscape of youth soccer. Through my experiences as a player, coach, recruiter, and, most importantly, a soccer dad, I aimed to share insights that can make this journey more rewarding and less daunting.

Reflecting on our chapters, we began by laying the foundations of youth soccer. We explored the importance of understanding age-specific needs, creating a positive environment, and instilling basic ball control and game rules. We also discussed essential equipment for young players, emphasizing the need for cost-effective solutions.

In the second chapter, we delved into structuring effective training sessions for different age groups. From U6 to U10, we covered how to keep sessions engaging, introduce basic skills and tactics, and maintain a balance between drills and fun games. We also touched on the role of technology in enhancing training.

Chapter three focused on developing core soccer skills. We looked at dribbling, passing, shooting, defensive skills, and goalkeeping basics. Each section provided practical drills and exercises to help young players build a strong technical foundation.

In chapter four, we explored the mental aspects of soccer. We discussed building mental resilience, handling game-day pressure, visualization techniques, staying motivated, and dealing with setbacks and failures. These elements are crucial for developing well-rounded players who can handle the ups and downs of the sport.

We then moved on to position-specific training in chapter five. We broke down the roles and responsibilities of forwards, midfielders, defenders, and goalkeepers, providing tailored drills and strategies to excel in each position.

Chapter six was all about fun and engaging drills. We introduced game-based drills, interactive challenges, and mini-games to keep young players excited about practice while honing their skills.

In chapter seven, we shared inspirational stories and role models. From soccer prodigies to female soccer stars and professional coaches, these stories highlighted the importance of perseverance, hard work, and resilience. We also included motivational quotes to inspire players, coaches, and parents alike.

Chapter eight focused on the role of family involvement in youth soccer. We discussed ways to encourage family participation, at-home soccer activities, discussing soccer values at home, and supporting your child without overstepping. Soccer is not just a game; it's a family affair that can bring everyone closer.

Chapter nine addressed common challenges in youth soccer. We provided strategies for keeping young players engaged, balancing fun and learning, simplifying complex soccer concepts, and handling parental expectations and pressure.

Finally, in chapter ten, we shared advanced tips and techniques. We covered advanced dribbling drills, tactical awareness, physical fitness, using data and analytics, preparing for competitive matches, injury prevention and recovery, and long-term player development pathways. These insights are designed to help young players take their game to the next level.

As you close this book, I hope you feel equipped and inspired to support your young soccer players. Whether you are a parent, coach, or player, remember that the journey is as important as the destination. Celebrate the small victories, learn from the setbacks, and cherish the moments on and off the field.

Encourage your child to enjoy the game, make friends, and develop a love for soccer that will last a lifetime. Keep the focus on learning and personal growth rather than just winning trophies. The skills and values learned through soccer will benefit them in all areas of life.

Now, I encourage you to take what you've learned and put it into practice. Organize family soccer days, engage in fun drills at home, and support your child through their soccer journey. Stay involved, stay positive, and most importantly, have fun.

Thank you for joining me on this journey through youth soccer. I wish you and your young soccer players all the best in your endeavors. May the love for the game continue to grow and bring joy to your lives.

Coach, Mentor, Recruiter, and Soccer Dad,

Matthew Eric

REFERENCES

Soccer Drive. (n.d.). *Soccer drills: Search by age & category*. Retrieved from https://www.soccerdrive.com/soccer-drills

360Player. (n.d.). *8 ways to communicate effectively in youth sports*. Retrieved from https://www.360player.com/blog/8-ways-to-communicate-effectively-in-youth-sports

Ollie Sports. (n.d.). *7 steps for creating a positive soccer team culture*. Retrieved from https://www.olliesports.com/post/7-steps-for-creating-a-positive-soccer-team-culture

Complete Soccer Guide. (n.d.). *Soccer ball control drills*. Retrieved from https://completesoccerguide.com/soccer-ball-control-drills/

Open Goaaal USA. (n.d.). *8 best U6 soccer drills for player development*. Retrieved from https://opengoaaalusa.com/blogs/news/u6-soccer-drills

Soccer Drive. (n.d.). *U8 soccer drills*. Retrieved from https://www.soccerdrive.com/soccer-drills/age-level/u8

TOCA Football. (n.d.). *How TOCA Football's soccer technology is shaping future*. Retrieved from https://www.tocafootball.com/journal-post/soccer-technology

Beyond Pulse. (n.d.). *6 strategies for adding more play to youth sports training*. Retrieved from https://learn.beyondpulse.com/blog/strategies-for-adding-more-play/

Rise FC Soccer. (n.d.). *10 essential soccer dribbling drills for youth and beginners*. Retrieved from https://www.risefcsoccer.com/soccer-dribbling-drills-for-youth/

Jersey Watch. (n.d.). *10 soccer passing drills to improve ball movement*. Retrieved from https://www.jerseywatch.com/blog/simple-youth-soccer-passing-drills

Blayze. (n.d.). *5 drills to improve shooting accuracy*. Retrieved from https://blayze.io/blog/soccer/5-drills-to-improve-shooting-accuracy

Rise FC Soccer. (n.d.). *9 soccer defending drills for defensive play*. Retrieved from https://www.risefcsoccer.com/youth-soccer-defending-drills/

National Center for Biotechnology Information. (2021). *Building resilience through sport in young people with mental health issues*. Retrieved from https://www.ncbi.nlm.nih.gov/pmc/articles/PMC8319951/

Positive Psychology. (n.d.). *Boosting mental toughness in young athletes.* Retrieved from https://positivepsychology.com/mental-toughness-for-young-athletes/

Upper Mentality. (n.d.). *Pre-game routines for mental preparation in youth soccer.* Retrieved from https://uppermentality.ca/f/pre-game-routines-for-mental-preparation-in-youth-soccer

Coaching American Soccer. (n.d.). *Visualization for soccer.* Retrieved from https://coachingamericansoccer.com/psychology/visualization-for-soccer/

SportsEdTV. (n.d.). *How to score more in soccer: Drills every forward must practice.* Retrieved from https://sportsedtv.com/blog/how-to-score-more-in-soccer-drills-every-forward-must-practice

Soccer Interaction Academy. (n.d.). *Midfielder's ultimate guide: Roles, tactics, and star players.* Retrieved from https://soccerinteraction.academy/en/soccer-academy-blog/midfielders-roles-tactics

Be Your Best. (n.d.). *A guide to defensive positioning in soccer.* Retrieved from https://www.beyourbest.com/insight/a-guide-to-defensive-positioning-in-soccer

Science for Sport. (n.d.). *Goalkeeper training: 5 key movement skills and how to train them.* Retrieved from https://www.scienceforsport.com/goalkeeper-training-5-key-movement-skills-and-how-to-train-them/

Soccer Drive. (n.d.). *7 fun U8 soccer drills for kids.* Retrieved from https://www.soccerdrive.com/blog/1/7-fun-u8-soccer-drills-kids

Soccer Drive. (n.d.). *U10 soccer drills.* Retrieved from https://www.soccerdrive.com/soccer-drills/age-level/u10

SEFA Soccer. (n.d.). *Youth soccer training: Benefits of small-sided games.* Retrieved from https://sefasoccer.com/small-sided-games/

Medium. (n.d.). *The extraordinary journey: How Lionel Messi overcame struggles to achieve legendary success.* Retrieved from https://medium.com/illumination/the-extraordinary-journey-how-lionel-messi-overcame-struggles-to-achieve-legendary-success-6eeb86816e4c

NPR. (2020, November 9). *Soccer star Megan Rapinoe on equal pay, and what the U.S. flag means to her.* Retrieved from https://www.npr.org/2020/11/09/933018609/soccer-star-megan-rapinoe-on-equal-pay-and-what-the-u-s-flag-means-to-her

Soccer Coaches. (n.d.). *Pep Guardiola - The tactical mastermind.* Retrieved from https://soccer-coaches.com/pep-guardiola-tactical-mastermind/

Soccer.com. (n.d.). *40 inspirational soccer quotes for players and coaches.*

Retrieved from https://www.soccer.com/guide/motivational-soccer-quotes

National Center for Biotechnology Information. (2021). *The role of parental involvement in youth sport experience.* Retrieved from https://www.ncbi.nlm.nih.gov/pmc/articles/PMC8391271/

Be Your Best. (n.d.). *Fun soccer games for kids.* Retrieved from https://www.beyourbest.com/insight/fun-soccer-games-for-kids

KidsHealth. (n.d.). *Teaching your child to be a good sport.* Retrieved from https://kidshealth.org/en/parents/sportsmanship.html

Delusion Group. (n.d.). *Understanding and preventing burnout as a youth